DESERT CROSSINGS

Transformed by Tribulations

ROBERT PETTERSON

COVENANT BOOKS

First Edition 2010

Copyright © 2010 by Robert Petterson
All rights reserved

ISBN 978-0615427225

Published by
Covenant Books
Printed in the USA

Design by
Erik Peterson & Project o3
www.projecto3.com

Comments may be directed
to the author via internet at:
robertpetterson@msn.com

TABLE OF CONTENTS

To Joyce
Beloved Companion
& Fellow Traveler

To Rachael
Beloved Daughter
& Future Hope

You have both given me grace,
encouragement and inspiration
in my desert crossings.

ACKNOWLEDGMENTS

The wisest man who ever lived wrote in Ecclesiastes 1:9, "What has been will be again, what has been done will be done again; there is nothing new under the sun." If I say anything of value, it is out of the rich reservoir of what has been poured into me by a lifetime of mentors and friends. Though I mention a handful here, I am indebted to so many more.

I am most grateful to my Lord Jesus Christ who crossed the desert of tribulation so that I might gain a paradise of eternal life. I stand in awe of multitudes of God's people who have crossed deserts on the way to their Promised Lands, especially the desert prophets and fathers.

Again, I acknowledge my dear wife Joyce who has been my companion and encourager in desert crossings together. I am indebted to my daughter Rachael who challenges me to live with integrity, while remaining relevant to a post-modern culture.

I am also grateful to my assistant and friend, William Barnett who has trekked deserts with me, and who will not let me rest until the books in my mind are put down on paper.

I am indebted to Dave and Patti Berg, for giving me their bit of Wisconsin paradise as a sanctuary for writing. Likewise, I greatly appreciate Basil and Patti Anderson for extending the hospitality of their beach condo in Montego Bay for further reflection and writing.

I am grateful to Dr. Bob Palmer, Mr. John Hunter and a host of other friends who have encouraged and even pushed me to publish this work.

Finally, I am amazed at the generosity of the elders, pastors, staff, and congregation of Covenant Presbyterian Church of Naples, Florida for giving me the time and resources to share with you what I have taught them. I am most blessed to be the Senior Pastor of a wonderfully supportive church.

FOREWORD

"Be not careless in deeds, nor confused in words, nor
rambling in thought."

                                        Marcus Aelius Aurelius

Mahatma Gandhi famously quipped, "I like your Christ, I do not like your Christians. Your Christians are unlike your Christ." In a single line he exposed the great scandal of Christianity. By every measure, the majority of those who profess Christ do not think, talk, or live like him.

In a postmodern world, this is a disaster. Christian apologist Ravi Zacharias asks, "How do you reach a generation that listens with its eyes?" We live in an age when people respond to what they see rather than to what they are told.

The Bible makes a promise: those redeemed by Christ will be transformed into his likeness. When Christians aren't like Christ, the watching world dismisses their faith as fraudulent. On his deathbed, existentialist John Paul Sartre confessed, "My philosophy has not worked." How tragic for a dying Christian to admit, "My Faith did not work. I have not become like Christ."

The scandal of Christianity begs the question: how, then, will Christians be transformed into the likeness of Christ? The purpose of this book is to give at least one biblical answer.

But beware of thinking that the answers in this book will transform you. Transformation doesn't come from acquiring more knowledge. Voltaire wrote, "The multitude of books is making us ignorant." St. Paul describes a lot of Christians as "...always learning but never coming to a knowledge of the truth." (2 Timothy 3:7 KJV) To paraphrase the same apostle, they have a form of godliness without the power (2 Timothy 3:5). Mere knowledge is powerless to produce spiritual reality.

The main thrust of this book is simple: you will never look like Christ until you look at Christ. St. Paul said, "And we, who with unveiled faces all reflect the Lord's glory are being transformed into his likeness with ever-increasing glory..." (2 Corinthians 3:17) Another apostle promises, "But we know that when he appears, we shall be like him, for we shall see him as he is." (1 John 3:2) We are transformed by our focus.

The second thrust of this book is borne of sad reality: we do not focus on our Creator because we are too focused on the things he created. As a result, we are conformed to the things of the creation rather than transformed into the image of the Creator.

We might wish that knowing these two facts would be enough to change reality. St. Paul exhorts, "Do not conform any longer to the pattern of this world, but be transformed by the renewing of your mind..." (Romans 12:2) But acquiring Bible knowledge does not in itself transform minds. If that were so, this generation of overfed Evangelicals would be the most transformed in history. Yet nothing could be further from the truth.

The final thrust of this book is that your sufferings reveal the inadequacies of creation by putting you on deserts that can't quench your thirst, feed your hunger, or offer shelter from storms. In desperation, you are driven back into the arms of the Creator you have neglected. As you again gaze at him, you will be transformed into his likeness with ever-increasing glory.

We have chosen a metaphor to describe this process: the desert crossing. The Bible repeatedly reminds us that heroes of the faith were forged in the crucible of the desert. Even Jesus was not spared his own desert sojourn.

In this study of the Exodus, we will see how God uses deserts to transform people. We will discover a principle that has been sadly ignored by an increasingly postmodern church: The road to your Promised Land must always go through the desert.

The Sinai is a string of deserts. Each has unique challenges that distinguish it from the others. In the same way, our transformation is a gradual process that requires us to cross many deserts. And so each chapter of Desert Crossings is designed to take you on another desert that is common to human suffering. Each is also borne out of my own crucible of suffering. As you enter the pages of this book, I remind the reader of a warning from St. Augustine's Confessions:

"The words here are concepts. You must go through the experiences."

Robert Petterson
November 2010

TRANSFORMED BY TRIBULATIONS

INTRODUCTION

"The philosophers have only interpreted the world in various ways. The point, however, is to change it."

Karl Marx

INTO THE FURNACE

There are few hellholes on earth more desolate than the string of deserts that form the Sinai. Satellite photos show it to be a sun-baked emptiness as barren as a moonscape.

With little humidity to block the sun's rays, the Sinai sizzles with double the solar radiation of more humid places. As a result, it loses almost as much heat at night. Temperatures soar above 120° Fahrenheit during the day and plunge below freezing after sunset.

Windswept and treeless mountains anchor its southern regions. Their barren peaks plunge into deep ravines where predators lurk in the shadows of an endless maze of hard rock canyons.

Blazing-hot deserts make up the northern Sinai. Those who set out across these badlands enter nature's furnace of affliction. Desert quicksand has been known to swallow whole caravans. Sands, driven at bullet speed by violent winds, disintegrate travelers with the full force of a sandblaster until nothing is left but their sandals. The Sinai is inhospitable and uninhabitable, offering only hunger, thirst and death to those who dare enter its savage domains.

Yet God called some three million sons and daughters of Abraham out of Egypt on an epic forty-year trek across the Sinai. He could have led them along the Mediterranean Sea. That would have been a romp in the park compared to the brutality of the Sinai.

On the surface, this desert crossing seems so sadistic. In fact, it is a severe mercy designed to forge a great nation out of a ragtag rabble. Had their exodus been a short jaunt along the sea, they would have arrived unprepared to seize the Promised Land from six million heavily armed Canaanites, many of them giants living in fortified cities. The Israelites would have faced certain annihilation.

Transformation comes in the furnace of affliction. History bears witness to the fact that those who changed the world were first transformed through seasons of suffering. Moses spent forty years being groomed as the Prince of Egypt. After his failed slave rebellion, he spent the next forty years as a fugitive on the

A Journey through the Pages of History
September 26-October 9, 2016
Dr. Bob Petterson, Host

Travel through 4,000 years in 12 days. Walk where God raised up kings and toppled empires. All of history is really *His* Story. Some is recorded in the Bible, the rest chiseled in the stones of Hittites, the ruins of ancient cities, and in scrolls and pottery left behind. Follow the route of Alexander the Great as he marched out from Macedonia to transform the world. Stand where Augustus turned a Roman republic into an Empire. Sail where Trojans, Greeks, Persians, Romans, Crusaders, and Ottomans moved mighty armadas. Walk in the footsteps of St. Paul and the Apostles. Sit in arenas where martyrs faced lions.

History will come alive through the inspirational lectures and informal chats with pastor, author, historian, and social commentator, Dr. Robert Petterson. The Bible will become more relevant than ever as we learn how past history effects events as current as tomorrow's headlines.

Itinerary

September 26: Depart USA

Departure flight from USA. Overnight on board the flight.

September 27: Thessaloniki, Greece

Arrive at Thessaloniki, Greece. You would be met and welcomed by your Greek guide. Transfer to your hotel in the heart of the always lively Greek co-capital of Thessaloniki. This evening you are invited for the welcome reception at your hotel. Overnight.
Hotel: Electra Palace

September 28: Thessaloniki, Greece

After a good night's sleep, a late morning start for our Thessaloniki tour where the New Testament books of I & II Thessalonians will come alive. Visit the old city ramparts; the newly excavated Forum, an ancient Roman monument which was transformed into a church, and the famous Via Egnatia, the road on which Paul walked to Thessaloniki. It was here in the synagogue that Paul "...reasoned with the Jews and the God-fearing Greeks." The afternoon will be free to enjoy a walk at the seaside or the Old Town of Thessaloniki where you will find beautiful places to try local specialties!
Meals: B

September 29: Philippi, Kavala, Alexandroupolis

This morning we drive to Philippi, where St. Paul delivered his first sermon in Europe, sowing the seeds of Christianity (Acts 16:12-18). Here St. Paul baptized a certain woman named Lydia, the first Christian convert in Europe. Visit the Roman Forum, and the prison where St. Paul and Silas were thrown. We will stand on the battlefield where Augustus defeated Cassius and Brutus, and changed a republic into an empire.

Following the route of Alexander the Great, we will continue to the modern port city of Kavala, ancient Neapolis, where St. Paul, accompanied by Silas, Luke and Timothy, first set foot in Europe. We will continue to Alexandroupolis the beautiful seaside town right before the borders. Dinner and overnight.
Hotel: Astir-Egnatia / Meals: B, D

September 30: Troas, Canakkale

Morning border crossing into Turkey; we cross the beautiful
Dardanelles and continue to Biblical Troas founded about 300BC by
one of the generals of Alexander the Great. During Apostle Paul's
Second Journey, it was from Troas that he received the Vision of the
"Macedonian call" to Europe. This is where Luke's account changes
from "they" to "we" (Acts 16:6-12) indicating that he joined Paul's
team at Troas. Returning from Macedonia during his third journey,
Paul was in Troas for a week when a young man Eutychus fell from
the third loft as Paul preached. Continue to Canakkale, the site of the
famous battle of Gallipoli where the Allies suffered one of the worst
defeats in World War I and the Ottoman Empire died. Dinner and
overnight
Hotel: Kolin / Meals: B, D

October 01: Pergamum, Smyrna, Izmir

Continue to beautiful Pergamum, where we begin our journey of the
Seven Churches of the Book of Revelation. Pergamum rises high on a
hill as one nears the city of Bergama. Coming down the mountain we
will head on to Izmir, which stands on the ancient site of Smyrna,
which John referred to as the poor, persecuted church that God
announced was rich due to their faithfulness amidst their suffering
(Revelation 2:8-11). Visit to church of Smyrna, the ruins of the
Roman agora—the market place—take the visitor back to apostolic
days. The citadel, known as the Kadifekale, built by Alexander the
Great on Mount Pagos (elevation 525 ft.), will be viewed overlooking
the city. Back to Izmir for dinner and overnight.
Hotel: Hilton Izmir / Meals: B, D

October 02: Thyatira, Sardis, Philadelphia

Our first visit today is at Thyatira, once a busy trading center and
famous in dyeing of purple clothes. Thyatira is one of the Seven
Churches mentioned in the Book of Revelation that tolerated the false
prophetess, Jezebel (Rev 1:11, 2:18-29). Continue to Sardis, another
of the Seven Churches. Jesus told Sardis, "...I know your deeds; you
have a reputation of being alive, but you are dead." Rev 3:1. Coins
were minted and dyeing of wool originated in Sardis. You will be
impressed by the massive scale of the Temple of Artemis, by the

white marble Royal Road, by the gymnasium and by the Synagogue. Continue to Philadelphia also one of the Seven Churches Rev 3:7-13. Christ told those who overcame that He would write upon them "the name of my God, and the name of the city of my God, which is New Jerusalem Rev 3:12. Today not much is left to mark the spot. You will see an ancient wall and the remains of a Byzantine basilica. We continue to Pamukkale for dinner and overnight.
Hotel: Pam Thermal / Meals: B, D

October 03: Laodicea and Ephessos, Kusadasi

Morning visit Laodicea; the Christians of Laodicea, one of the Seven Churches (Rev 3:14-22), were chastised for being lukewarm, "You are neither cold nor hot" (Rev 3.15) and for being too comfortable incorporating pagan and Christian beliefs. In the famous Scripture from Revelation (3:20-21), Jesus says to the Laodicean Church "Behold, I stand at the door and knock..." Today, there are many acres of ruins to see, including the stadium and columned streets.

Afternoon, visit the most impressive biblical site of our trip: Ephesus where Paul first came on his second journey (Acts 18:19-21). Ephesus was one of the most beautiful cities of ancient world and its former glory can still be appreciated today from its well- preserved streets, temples, fountains, public baths, terraced houses and theatres. Paul returned to Ephesus on his third journey, staying and preaching for a period of about two years, where "special miracles" were wrought (Acts19:120, 20:20). Dinner and overnight in Kusadasi
Hotel: Korumar / Meals: B, D

October 04: Embark Cruise ship, Patmos

Embark our cruise ship, the Celestyal Olympia; sail by noon. Early afternoon arrival on the island of Patmos. It was here in Patmos where John the Divine, while in exile, wrote the Apocalyptic Revelations, which constitute the last part of the New Testament. Disembark and meet for the Shore experience on Patmos Island. The tour takes you to the monastery of St. John, which still keeps its character of a medieval fortress. Inside the walls you will be able to admire the Byzantine wealth of the Christian Orthodox religion while from its high ground you will have the most stunning panoramic view of the luminous sea. After the visit of St. John Monastery, we proceed to the

Grotto – the Holy Cave of Apocalypse where St John is said to have had the vision of fire and brimstone and dictated the book of Revelation. Return to the Port of Patmos – free time.
Meals: B, L, D

October 05: Cruise: Rhodes

All day call at the port where the Collossus was standing at the ancient times…just walking distance to the medieval town, the same streets the Knights of Rhodos were walking and living. Our tour takes us to the Bay of St Paul under the shadow of the impressive Acropolis of Lindos; this is where Paul docked with his boat on the way back to Jerusalem.
Meals: B, L, D

October 06: Cruise: Crete and Santorini

This morning we dock at the legendary island of Crete, land of Minoan civilization, home of Zorbas the Greek

Afternoon call at the volcano island of Santorini; take the cable car on your own to visit the top of the island and enjoy the panoramic view of the famous Caldera or join an optional shore excursion to visit the island (USD 85 pp)
Meals: B, L, D

October 07: Athens

Morning dock Pireaus, Athens tour. See Constitution Square (Syntagma), the House of Parliament, the memorial to the Unknown Soldier and the University, the Academie and the National Library. Driving down Herodes Atticus street and the Avzones in their picturesque uniforms and the Presidential Palace. On your way to the Acropolis you will see the Panathenaic Stadium (where the first Olympic Games of the modern era held in 1896), the Temple of Olympia Zeus and Hadrian's Arch. On the Acropolis mount, you will visit the architectural masterpieces of the Golden Age of Athens: The Propylee, the Temple of Athena Nike, the Erechtheion and finally the Parthenon – the monument that "puts order in the mind" and "is harmony between material and spirit" Beneath the Acropolis is the Areopagus or Mars Hill. This is where St. Paul made his famous "Men of Athens" speech revealing a considerable knowledge of the

Greek philosophy and character. Dinner and overnight in Athens
Hotel. Royal Olympic / Meals: B

October 08: Ancient Corinth tour

Following breakfast this morning we travel west with a rest stop and photos at the Corinth Canal. We then travel to the ancient city of Corinth, another treat for the New Testament scholar. Corinth is the city that inspired many of Paul's most familiar letters. See the Archaeological

Museum, the Market Place, the Bema, and the Temples. To enjoy a devotional in the midst of the ruins of the church of Corinth and see the pillars, steps, and public worship place where Paul preached will enhance your understanding and love of I & II Corinthians. The ruins of this important cultural center are fascinating as we walk along the stone path that the Apostle Paul walked. The engineering skill and intellect of these people are evident in the water systems that still flow from ancient to modern day. Our guide will be sure to show you the room dedicated to the medical care of that period. Return to Athens for our farewell dinner at a beautiful Greek restaurant overlooking illuminated Acropolis
Meals: B, D

October 09: Departure

Transfer to Athens airport for our flight back home!
Meals: B

Included Features

TRANSFERS & PORTERAGE:

Roundtrip transfers between airport and hotels, including assistance by our tour representative upon arrival and departure. Porterage of one (1) average sized piece of luggage per person.

ACCOMMODATIONS:

Sep 27 – 29	2	Thessaloniki	Hotel Electra Palace
Sep 29 – 30	1	Alexandroupolis	Hotel Astir-Egnatia
Dep 30–Oct 1	1	Canakkale	Kolin
Oct 1 –2	1	Izmir	Hilton Izmir
Oct 2-3	1	Pamukkale	Pam Thermal
Oct 3 – 4	1	Kusadasi	Korumar
Oct 4 – 7	3	Sailing	Celestyal Olympia
Oct 7 – 9	2	Athens	Royal Olympic

MEALS:

Breakfast daily / 2 lunches / 9 dinners / Welcome cocktail party

SIGHTSEEING:

Comprehensive touring via luxury air-conditioned vehicle including all entrance fees to sites visited and the services of a government licensed English-Speaking guide at the disposal of the group as per the attached suggested land itinerary. Shore excursions included are: Patmos (Monastery of John) and Rhodes, Lindos – port of St. Paul.

Also included are all gratuities to guides, drivers and ship board personnel

Tour Prices

- $4,365.00 per person predicated on double occupancy
- Price includes all land portions of trip
- Minimum of 30 passengers required
- Single Supplement $1,090.00
- A deposit of $500 per person payable to Regency Travel by check or credit card is needed to secure a reservation. $250 of the deposit is nonrefundable

Not Included

- Airline travel
- Visa to enter Turkey which can be obtained on line prior to travel.
- Regency Travel will assist in making airline reservations and obtaining the visa for anyone requesting the service.
- Shore excursions in Crete and Santorini
- Expenses of a personal nature
- Charges for items not on menus in hotels and restaurant
- Alcoholic and soft beverages and wine with meals when not included

Contact Information

Chris Allan
Regency Travel
chrisallan@embarqmail.com
Phone: (239) 596-6222 or (239) 641-4431

Cindy Esposito
Covenant Church
Phone: (239) 597-3464

backside of a desert. In the savagery of the Sinai, Moses was transformed into a desert firebrand who changed history. His life proves that palaces may produce princes, but deserts forge prophets.

OUT OF EGYPT

The furnace must be hot indeed to burn away the impurities of Egypt. Abraham and his descendants could not resist the seductions of Egypt. When famine ravaged Canaan, Abraham fled there to find food. The sons of Jacob went there, seeking grain during another famine. After the Babylonians decimated Israel, the survivors of that holocaust escaped to Egypt. Joseph, Mary, and Jesus also found refuge in Egypt.

Perhaps it was the Nile that seduced the desert folk of the Middle East. While they depended on sporadic rains for their survival, the Nile rolled through Egypt with monotonous predictability. It produced one of the richest breadbaskets of the world. Cattle grew fat along the Nile, as did the Egyptians who harvested its abundance. The desert killed and the Nile gave life. Desert nomads barely eked out an existence while Egyptians lived in luxury.

But the Nile also exacted a heavy toll for its largess. It demanded the worship of those it fed, becoming the chief god among Egyptian deities. The creatures that came from the Nile were worshipped as gods, as were the pharaohs who built civilization along its banks. As each god-king tried to surpass past pharaohs, an endless supply of workers was needed. The god-kings saw the descendants of Abraham as an unending source of slave labor. For 400 years, the Nile that fed the Jews also devoured them.

Yet Egypt is powerfully addictive. Even its slaves found it almost impossible to shake its seductions. The same Israelites who rejoiced when they escaped their bondage, looked back nostalgically during their desert crossings, Repeatedly they lamented,

> "If only we had meat to eat! We remember the fish we ate in Egypt at no cost—also the cucumbers, melons, leeks, onions and garlic."
>
> *Numbers 11:4&5*

Could there be a more delusional statement? The truth is: the fish from the Nile cost them everything. Egypt stole their faith, freedom, and dignity. The genocidal policies of Egypt dismantled their families and fed their babies to the Nile crocodiles.

Beware of Egypt's seductions. They are so powerful that they make us forget the ravages of their slavery. Egypt is not so much a nation in Africa as it is a state of mind. We postmodern Christians are seduced by our own versions of Egypt. Then we are enslaved to their pleasures. Like ancient Israelites, we delude ourselves into thinking that we partake of them at no cost to our families, our faith, or ourselves.

Until we understand the slavery hidden within the seductions of Egypt, we will never be thankful for the severe mercy of God in taking us out of there, and into the furnace of our own Sinai. No one understood both Egypt and the need for the desert cure better than St. Augustine of Hippo. This Desert Father brilliantly exposed Egypt's deception.

EGYPT UNMASKED

As a young man, Augustine wasted his youth in a reckless

pursuit of pleasure. He later wrote, "I drank the cup of lust to its last bitter dregs." He compared those lost years to a sojourn in Egypt. Even after his conversion, he struggled with an addiction to his Egypt—the pleasures of Roman life. So he went "cold turkey" by fleeing to the deserts of his native North Africa. There he devoted himself to the study of St. Paul's Epistle to the Romans. In the first chapter, he discovered the mother of all sins:

> "For although they knew God, they neither glorified him as God nor gave thanks...They exchanged the truth of God for a lie, and worshipped and served created things rather than the Creator—who is forever praised. Amen."
>
> *Romans 1:21&25*

Augustine says that the root of every sin is our decision to worship creation and its creatures. Above all, we deify ourselves as the chief creature. This was the original sin in Eden. Adam and Eve were presented with a choice: either they would find their hope and comfort in their Creator or turn to the forbidden fruit. When they took that fruit, they chose creation over their Creator. They exchanged the truth of God for Satan's lie: "God knows that when you eat of it... you will be like God." (Genesis 3:4)

Every choice boils down to whether we will find our pleasure, security and hope in creation or our Creator. Augustine says that this is the great issue of Egypt. As long as we depend on the Nile for life, its pharaohs to feed us, and its civilization to sustain us, we worship creation and creatures instead of the Creator.

But creation and creatures are harsh gods. Forbidden fruit brings death and Egypt enslaves. God will not allow us to substitute his glory with the worship of creation, its creatures, and their creations. Augustine reminds us of St. Paul's warning:

> "But the wrath of God is being revealed from heaven against
> all the godlessness and wickedness of men who suppress
> the truth by their wickedness."
>
> *Romans 1:18*

How is God now pouring out this wrath from heaven? Augustine tells us that he turns us over to all kinds of sins. Twenty-seven are mentioned in the first chapter of Romans: everything from idolatry to malice to murder. The Bishop of Hippo concludes that God's judgment on sin is sin. But only one sin is the cause of all other sins: putting our hope in creation and its creatures rather than the Creator.

Egypt is a different place for each of us. It may be a person we cling to, a job that we depend on, a child through whom we live vicariously, a talent that feeds our need for applause, an addiction that helps us forget our pain, social status that deludes us into feeling superior, or even religion that makes us feel holier than others. Remember, Adam and Eve even found their Egypt in the Garden of Eden.

St. Augustine reminds us that Egypt is not a country in North Africa, but any place where the adulterous heart flees for refuge instead of turning to God.

THE DESERT CURE

The Bishop of Hippo argued that the desert is the only cure for Egypt. When he fled to the desert, he was part of a movement that swept through the ancient Church. Thousands fled to deserts seeking spiritual transformation. Their desert crossings are chronicled in one of the classics of Early Christianity: the Sayings of the Desert Fathers.

One of those desert fathers was Abba Arsenius. This Roman nobleman was a tutor to the children of Emperor Theodosius. He enjoyed the pleasures of the palace, but his soul was empty. So he cried out, "God lead me in the way of salvation." A voice whispered back, "Arsenius, flee from this world and you will be saved." He quit his post and sailed to Alexandria in Egypt. Again he cried out to God, and a voice came back, "Flee alone to the desert, and pray."

Among city crowds, the Desert Fathers heard only the hollowness of human conversation. In desert solace they found the holiness of silence. In their aloneness they were forced to embrace their Creator for companionship. In the barrenness of the desert, they had to depend on him for food, water, and shelter.

Their desert meditations birthed breathtaking prayers, soaring worship, and towering theological treatises that would become the bulwark of Christianity. Many, like Athanasius, John Chrysostom, and Augustine, returned from their desert crossings as transformed saints who changed society and history.

The desert is still the cure for Egypt. But, like Egypt, the desert is not so much a spot on a map as a life situation. By definition, the desert is the place of desolation. If you find no relief from soul thirst, you are in a desert. Some individuals are as barren as deserts. So are many marriages, families, churches, and communities. Israel Zangwill lamented, "New York City is the great stone desert." Perhaps you are in a desert of your own making. James Lovelock said, "It is much easier to create a desert than a forest." But God is pleased to redeem the deserts of your making by turning them into places of transformation. Which begs the inescapable question: how does the desert do its work?

TRANSFORMED IN THE DESERT

Remember, Egypt calls us to turn from our Creator and find our pleasure and sustenance in creation and its creatures. For the ancient Hebrews, seduction was in the abundance of the Nile. Our seductions are far more diverse and sophisticated. Ours make the luxuries and diversions of ancient Egypt pale by comparison. St. Paul warns those of us who are addicted to the empty pleasures of our postmodern Egypt,

> "Do not conform any longer to the pattern of this world, but be transformed by the renewing of your mind..."
>
> *Romans 12:2*

When his brothers first came to Egypt, they didn't even recognize Joseph because he dressed, talked, and walked like an Egyptian. Spend enough time in Egypt and you will conform to it. After 400 years there, the descendants of Jacob's sons resembled Egyptians more than they did Abraham. So God took them out of Egypt and into the Sinai furnace of affliction. How does the desert transform those conformed to Egypt? St. Paul unlocks the secret in his Second Letter to the Corinthian Christians:

> "Now the Lord is the Spirit, and where the Spirit of the Lord is, there is freedom. And we, who with unveiled faces all reflect the Lord's glory are being transformed into his likeness with ever-increasing glory..."
>
> *2 Corinthians 3:17&18*

In the wider context of these words, Paul is reminding his readers of how Moses had the rare privilege of looking directly at God. The glory of God lit up his face. Everyone who saw his countenance knew that Moses had been in God's presence. But the longer he was away from that presence, the more the glory faded until it vanished. So Moses put a veil over his face to keep others from watching the glory fade.

But Paul tells New Testament believers that Christ dwells in us. Filled with his presence and focusing on his person, we walk with "unveiled faces" because the glory never fades. We "are being transformed into his likeness with ever-increasing glory."

The desert transforms because it's that part of creation incapable of sustaining life. In this barren place, we are reduced to helplessness. Our only hope of survival is to look to our Creator for everything. St. Paul would say "amen" because transformation can only come when we behold God's glory.

This is why God brings plagues on our Egypt and strips it bare, just as he did in the ancient land of the Nile. Are you in the desert furnace of tribulation? Maybe those things, in which you have put your trust, have been visited with a plague. Perhaps your life has been stripped bare and secret sins have been exposed. Or your marriage is desolate, and you don't know what to do next. Or the economy has devoured your savings. Or your desert is some illness. Or the partner who sustained you is gone.

Don't lose heart. A gracious God has called you to the severe mercy of an exodus. Like the ancient Israelites, you will be tempted to complain that the desert crossing is a barren and bitter place compared to the comforts of Egypt. But, when you feel the desert sting, remember that God has redeemed you from the seductions and slaveries of Egypt. Now he is taking you to a Promised Land. St. Paul describes it this way:

"For those God foreknew, he also predestined to be conformed to the image of his Son, that he might be the
firstborn among many brothers. And those he predestined,
he also called; those he called, he also justified; those he
justified, he also glorified."

Romans 8:28&30

One day you will be just like Jesus Christ. Then you will
no longer think, talk, or walk like an Egyptian. But between
Egypt and the Promised Land there are deserts that must be
crossed. In your desert crossing you will discover that the things
of creation cannot get you to the other side. You will be forced
to cling desperately and tightly to your Creator. As you draw
close to him, you will behold his glory.

You may go through several deserts before you get to your
Promised Land. Each will deliver its unique brand of pain
that will force you to run to your Creator. But, in each desert,
there will be new transformation. Sometimes it will be barely
noticeable, and at other times it will be monumental. But it will
bring "ever-increasing glory."

Moses fled Egypt as a murderer. It was in the desert that the
failed prince became God's prophet. David became a Psalmist
and warrior in the desert. Elijah came out of the desert to spark
a revival. John the Baptist prepared the way for the Lord in the
desert. Jesus defeated Satan in the desert, and then left it to
redeem the world. After his conversion experience, St. Paul
spent three years with Jesus in the desert in order to become
a missionary to the world. And a ragtag rabble of whining,
complaining, and rebellious ex-slaves were transformed into
a unified nation of spiritual warriors during forty years of
desert crossings. They came out of the Sinai to seize a kingdom

and change the course of history.

Do you want to be transformed into the image of your Savior? Would you like to be a transforming force in your world? Then embrace the desert crossing. Each of the following chapters presents a different desert that has been crossed by millions. Perhaps you have already crossed some of them. Maybe you are crossing one of them right now. You will most likely cross all of them before you are changed into Christ's likeness.

May the following stories of fellow trekkers inspire and encourage you to persevere until you are fully transformed!

CHOICES

DESERT 1

"Nobody ever did or will escape the consequences of his choices."

Alfred Montapert

"Herbie" was the sweetest little boy in the Oak Brook neighborhood of Indianapolis. He might have grown up to be an angel if his doting mother hadn't died when he was four years old. Instead, his harsh father turned him into a devil who would terrorize the depression era Midwest.

Brutalized at home, "Herbie" became a playground bully. By the time he was in the sixth grade, he was a back alley brawler and petty thief. A year later he dropped out of school and became a drifter. At age nineteen he was arrested for auto theft. The judge gave him probation on condition that he join the navy. He soon deserted and was dishonorably discharged. He got married, but his violent temper killed the romance.

After his divorce, "Herbie" and a buddy robbed a grocery store. He was sentenced to twenty years for armed robbery. As he entered the Indiana State Prison he snarled, "I will be the biggest S.O.B. you ever saw when I get out of here."

When he was paroled eight years later, he made good on his vow. His gang became the most prolific bank robbers in U.S. history. Their exploits captured the imagination of a nation mired in the Great Depression. His daring jailbreaks were the stuff of legend.

The public adored him as a modern day Robin Hood, but "Herbie" was a vicious sociopath who hobnobbed with notorious gangsters like "Pretty Boy" Floyd and "Baby Face" Nelson. FBI Director, J. Edgar Hoover declared him Public Enemy Number One and launched the biggest manhunt in American history to bring him to justice.

Maybe you remember "Herbie" by his full name: John Herbert Dillinger. Mary Dillinger's little angel had grown up to become "the meanest S.O.B. you ever saw."

Not long before he was betrayed by his girlfriend and killed in an FBI ambush, John Dillinger confided to a friend, "I can trace my life of crime back to when I was nine years old. I stole a quarter from my old man's wallet. I was scared he would find out and give me a beating. But I got away with it. After that, stealing was easy."

Little "Herbie" steals a quarter. It doesn't seem like a big deal at the time. But it leads to a lifetime of choices that create John Dillinger, Public Enemy Number One. No choice is insignificant. The ancient philosopher Pythagoras said, "Choices are the hinges of destiny." Albert Camus wrote, "Life is the sum of all your choices." John Dillinger would surely agree.

Many of us are in deserts that have been created by bad choices. It's no accident that the opening lines of Exodus are about choices. Understanding this transforming truth will spare you unnecessary desert crossings:

MONUMENTAL CONSEQUENCES ARE SHAPED BY MOMENTARY CHOICES.

Management guru Stephen Covey says, "While we are free to choose our actions, we are not free to choose the consequences of our actions." Who would have thought that a nine year-old boy's decision to steal a quarter would set in motion a life of crime that sidetracked a nation and left a trail of violence in its bloody wake?

In our lifetime, we will make millions of choices. Many are reflex responses, snap decisions, unconscious choices, impulsive actions, or thoughtless reactions. Most seem so insignificant that they hardly warrant a second thought. But those forgettable choices are the threads that weave the inescapable fabric of our lives.

The decision you face may be as simple as whether or not you will eat a second donut or get up an hour earlier to pray. But those momentary choices are shaping a character that will decide how you make monumental decisions. Here are four principles from the opening verses of the Exodus story:

1. SLOW LEAKS WRECK MORE LIVES THAN BLOWOUTS

Eight verses into the Exodus story we see its first major player: "Then a new king who did not know Joseph came to power in Egypt." His subjects called him Pharaoh and worshipped him as a god. As ruler of the world's preeminent empire, he was the most powerful man on earth. He had barely ascended to the throne when he faced his first test of leadership:

> "'Look,' he said to his people, 'the Israelites have become much too numerous for us. Come, we must deal shrewdly with them or they will become even more numerous and, if war breaks out, will join our enemies, fight against us and leave our country."
>
> *Exodus 1:9&10*

Verse eight says that this new god-king "did not know Joseph." The book of Genesis tells the story of Joseph, the favorite son of Jacob. His jealous brothers sold him into Egyptian slavery. In a "rags-to-riches" story, he rose to become the nation's Prime Minister. His leadership saved Egypt from a famine. A grateful Pharaoh rewarded him by giving asylum to his refugee family when they came looking for food.

It's now centuries later. This new god-king doesn't remember who Joseph was, much less the promise a distant Pharaoh made 400 years earlier: that the descendants of Jacob's twelve sons could live as free herdsmen in their little corner of Egypt. That distant Pharaoh could not have imagined that Jacob's sons would spawn such a prolific birth rate:

"The Israelites were fruitful and multiplied greatly and became exceedingly numerous so that the land was full of them."

Exodus 1:7

In 400 years, this population of Jewish immigrants had exploded from twelve to some three million people. Their growth rate was at a tipping point. Within a few decades, they would outnumber the Egyptians.

Before you dismiss Pharaoh's panic, think of the angst in America over illegal aliens. There is a palpable fear that today's explosive immigrant population is spawning cataclysmic cultural, economic, political, and religious changes that will radically alter America's landscape. Frantic voices warn that our national security is at risk if the borders aren't closed and illegal immigrants sent packing.

The angst in the United States is a whimper compared to the anxiety raging across Europe where the Muslim population is exploding at such staggering rates that Islam could be the predominate culture within 50 years. Surely, we can understand the Pharaoh's panic in the face of the Jewish population explosion.

BLOWOUTS

But no one can justify his draconian response. Exodus 1:11-14 tells us that he made a monumental choice to enslave the Jews. The harshness of his new immigration policy is captured in these words: "...in all their hard labor, the Egyptians used them ruthlessly." Egypt's solution to population control was literally to work the Jewish men to death.

Their policy of attrition through brutal slave labor didn't work. The Jewish birthrate mushroomed. So, the god-king made another monumental decision, recorded in Exodus 1:16&21.

He ordered the systematic slaughter of all Jewish baby boys. It was history's first genocide.

It is said that Adolph Hitler loved little children and S.S. chief Himmler was a good family man. How can Heinrich Himmler or an Egyptian pharaoh preside over the genocide of babies and then go home to cuddle their own children? The answer is painfully simple: monstrous acts gradually and imperceptibly evolve out of a lifetime of lesser but increasingly sinister choices. A U.S. Safety Council report said that highway accidents caused by blown tires are usually from slow leaks, not sudden blowouts. Moral failures that wreck lives are almost always the same.

SLOW LEAKS

Ironically, Joseph planted the seeds of this genocide centuries earlier. During seven years of plentiful harvests, he filled the Pharaoh's granaries with wheat. In the ensuing seven years of famine, the Egyptians came to their god-king begging for food. On Joseph's advice, the Pharaoh fed them in exchange for their money. When they came again, he took their land and livestock. After the Pharaoh owned everything, the people became his slaves in order to feed at the government trough. All future pharaohs were the absolute masters of Egypt, holding the power of life and death over everyone.

Decisions made 400 years earlier, and reiterated through the centuries, determined the choices made by this pharaoh. Servants catered to his slightest whims from the time he was a baby. His tutors taught him that he was a god. He even married his own sister so that the DNA of mere mortals wouldn't pollute his bloodline. When he ascended to the throne, centuries of choices had programmed him to believe that his choices were a god's decision. If Egypt and its citizens were his to do with as he pleased, then surely it was his right to work Jewish slaves to death and order the genocide of their babies.

Eighty years later, when the desert prophet Moses came demanding that another pharaoh set the Jews free, why would he listen to the "god" of a slave people when he was the living god of the most powerful nation on earth?

Pharaoh's life and land were wrecked by slow leakage. When plagues later devastated Egypt, it wasn't a sudden blow-out. When the firstborn sons of Egypt were struck down by the Death Angel on Passover night, it wasn't a sudden blowout. When Pharaoh's army was drowned in the Red Sea, it wasn't a sudden blowout. How many times did that Pharaoh refuse to listen to Moses? How many times did he harden his heart against God's commands? In the end, Pharaoh was undone by slow leakage.

We are shocked when a 25-year marriage blows up in divorce, a respected preacher wrecks his ministry, a "family values" politician is destroyed by a moral failure, or a blue chip company careens into bankruptcy. The headlines make it seem like a sudden blowup. More likely each wreck was a result of the slow leakage of moral compromise in momentary choices over many years.

2. LIVE BY PRINCIPLE, AND MOST DECISIONS ARE ALREADY MADE.

In Exodus 1:15 we are introduced to Siphrah and Puah. The world hardly remembers these two women. Their lives are summed up in two words: Hebrew midwives. They were ordinary women who earned pennies a day assisting in the birth of slave babies. It must have been frightening for these ragged mid-wives to be ushered into the presence of a god-king who held the power of life and death over them. Their hearts surely skipped a beat when he issued this command from his lofty throne.

> "When you help the Hebrew women in childbirth and observe them on the delivery stool, if it is a boy, kill him; but if it is a girl, let her live."
>
> *Exodus 1:16*

This pharaoh's genocide was diabolically elegant in design: work the Jewish men to death, kill their baby boys, and leave their girls to marry Egyptian men. Pharaoh could have made Adolph Hitler's boast: "One day the Jews will be a distant memory."

You should not be shocked by Pharaoh's "final solution" to the Jewish problem. The U.S. Supreme Court's decision legalizing abortion in 1973 was the realization of Margaret Sanger's vision in the 1920s. Ms. Sanger was appalled at the birth rate of immigrants in the slums of New York City. She was as desperate as ancient pharaohs and contemporary Americans about immigrant populations. In her book Pivot of Civilization, she wrote that blacks, immigrants, and indigents are "...human weeds...reckless breeders...human beings who should never have been born..." Her solution was enforced birth control, sterilization, abortion, and infanticide. Thank God that Margaret Sanger wasn't a midwife in Egypt. But she did found Planned Parenthood, and some 50 million abortions later North Americans are killing babies on a scale that dwarfs the genocides of Egypt and Nazi Germany.

Siphrah and Puah had to make a choice: obey a pharaoh or stand on principle. In a postmodern culture we are increasingly hesitant to define what is "right" lest we offend some special interest group. Political correctness has hijacked moral imperative. In a relativistic society, we have created a morality of convenience for an age of softness. If we can't define very much as morally wrong, then we don't have to stand up for very much. But this wasn't complicated for Siphrah and Puah. We read in the Exodus story,

> "The midwives, however, feared God and did not do what
> the king of Egypt told them to do."
>
> *Exodus 1:17*

These simple midwives chose to disobey a pharaoh in order to keep Jewish babies alive. Their decision was forged by a principle that guided all their decisions: they feared God more than people.

There are only three motives for choice: pleasing or protecting yourself; pleasing or protecting yourself from others; or pleasing and finding protection in God. When they stood on the principle of fearing God, the decision for these midwives was easy. When we base our lives on this principle, ninety percent of our decisions are already made. By fearing God, Siphrah and Puah brought life to millions of unborn babies.

When you face costly choices remember these words from the Exodus story: "And because these midwives feared God, he gave them families of their own." (Exodus 1:21) You can't lose when you chose principles over pharaohs.

3. REASONABLE CHOICES ARE THE STUFF OF COMPROMISE

Outwitted by the midwives, Pharaoh responded by making another choice. He ordered the citizens of Egypt, "Every [Hebrew] boy that is born you must throw into the Nile..." (Exodus 1:22) Imagine turning your own people into a nation of baby-killers. Some eighty years later, God exacted a terrible retribution on the Egyptians for their complicity in mass murder. He sent his Death Angel to kill every firstborn Egyptian boy. Momentary choices do have monumental consequences.

In the second chapter of Exodus, we see a nameless couple. We know that they are descendants of Joseph's brother Levi, but they are destined to live and die in a slave's obscurity. This woman didn't know that she was carrying a liberator in her womb. It would have been reasonable for her to abort her baby, or to give him up to an Egyptian neighbor to drown. Others made such compromises to please their slave masters.

But this nameless slave woman hatched a desperate plan to save her boy. She put him in a basket and set him adrift on the Nile. She calculated that the current would take him down the river and into the bathing pool of the Pharaoh's daughter. What audacity! Did her family and friends whisper that it would never work? Didn't she know that there were hungry Nile crocodiles waiting for their daily feeding of Jewish babies? Even if the basket made it into the royal bathing pool, could they trust the daughter of a genocidal pharaoh? Even if the princess felt tenderness for a Jewish baby, wouldn't she raise him as an Egyptian prince? What would it matter if this slave woman's baby were saved if he grew up to be just another Egyptian slave master?

It was not a reasonable decision. But, if we limit our choices to what is reasonable or possible, only compromise is left. What motivated her to make such an impossible choice? We have to go to the New Testament to find the answer:

> "By faith Moses' parents hid him for three months after he was born because they saw that he was no ordinary child and they were not afraid of the king's edict."
>
> *Hebrews 11:23*

God rewards faith choices. Exodus two tells us that the boy's sister followed his basket down the Nile. She was there when Pharaoh's daughter found him. In a scenario that could only be drawn up in heaven's playbook, the princess of Egypt wondered how the baby would eat. Little Miriam stepped out of the bulrushes and offered, "Shall I go and get one of the Hebrew women to nurse the baby for you?" (Exodus 2:7)

For the next few years Moses' birth mother got to cuddle and nurse her own baby. Along with her milk, she gave him her faith. Though he was being reared as the Prince of Egypt, she gave him a precious gift: his identity as a child of God's covenant with Abraham. This nameless slave woman prepared a boy to liberate his people and change the history of the world. From her we learn that great choices are not always made on what is reasonable or possible. If we fail to grasp that, we are doomed to turn our world into a barren desert by the easy compromise that is so prevalent in our postmodern age.

4. EASY CHOICES NOW MAKE FOR A HARDER FUTURE

The Exodus narrative skips over the next forty years. Moses is now a middle-aged prince of Egypt. In our first glimpse of him, he is faced with a choice. He comes upon an Egyptian overseer beating a Jewish slave. As we watch Moses' response, we witness a man with conflicting emotions.

On the one hand, he is the son of a Jewish slave woman who taught him to have compassion for his people. So he can't ignore this slave beating. On the other hand, he is a son of the palace that schooled him to be a prince of Egypt. So he does what any pharaoh would do: in a fit of rage, he kills the overseer. It's the easy decision. Now forty years of conflicting emotions explode, and he tries to spark a slave uprising.

His impulsive revolution collapses. The Jews don't trust Moses because they see too much pharaoh in him. The Pharaoh no longer trusts his adopted grandson because he sees too much Jew in him. So we read in Exodus 2:15, "Moses fled and went to live in Midian." Moses is now a fugitive with a price on his head, hiding out in the badlands of the Sinai. He made the easy choice, and now he must endure the desert crossing. It will take forty years for the furnace of affliction to burn away the impurities of Egypt from this double-minded man.

Perhaps you are facing some momentary choices today. Maybe you are tempted to avoid the high cost of standing on biblical principle, even though the midwives who defied a pharaoh were rewarded with families of their own. Perhaps you think that choosing God's way is unreasonable, even though a nameless slave woman was rewarded for her impossible choice with a son who liberated her people. Some choices are easier in the short run. But pharaohs and princes discover that the slow leak of easy choices later wrecks lives. The Exodus story confirms the old proverb: easy now, harder later; harder now, easier later.

DESERT REFLECTIONS

After a lifetime of "easy" momentary choices, monumental consequences caught up with John "Herbie" Dillinger. He had become a bank robber to purchase Egypt's pleasures, only to make a desert of everything he touched.

Tragically, his desert did not transform him for the good because he didn't turn to his Creator for salvation. Days before he was gunned down outside a movie theater, he regretted that first "easy" choice to steal a quarter from his dad's wallet. But, by then, the slow leak was about to turn into a fatal blowout.

Hard choices are by definition hard. Jesus made the hard decision in the Garden of Gethsemane when he overcame his anguish and set his face toward the Cross. For him, Gethsemane was a desert crossing. Maybe you are in a desert today because of bad choices. Don't give in to John Dillinger's despair. Your desert can transform your life, if only you will turn to your Creator, Savior, and Sustainer Jesus Christ. His crossing from Gethsemane to Golgotha can turn your desert into a garden and use your tribulations to transform you into his image with ever-increasing glory.

WAITING

DESERT 2

"*The two most powerful warriors are patience and time.*"
Leo Tolstoy

He was seven years old when his family lost their Indiana farm. He had to drop out of school and go to work to help them pay off their debts. Two years later his beloved mother died. He would never recover from that heartbreak.

When he was twenty-two he started a business that went belly-up. Then he ran for the State Legislature and lost. He was hired to run a store, but fired a few months later. So he applied to law school only to be rejected. A friend loaned him money to try his hand at business again. Within a year he filed for bankruptcy.

He spent the next seventeen years paying off that debt.

He made another run at politics, and got a rare taste of success. The year that he took his seat in the State Legislature, he got engaged to the only woman he would ever love. But shortly afterwards she died of typhoid fever and he plunged into suicidal despair. He spent the next six months in bed. He would suffer debilitating bouts of depression for the rest of his life.

He recovered enough to get back into the political game, running for Speaker of the State House. He was soundly defeated. Two years later he ran for Elector and lost. His friends tried to cheer him up by pushing him into an arranged marriage. Her emotional instability and constant nagging would plague him for the twenty-three years of their loveless life together.

He ran for the U.S. Congress and lost again. Then his three year-old son Edward died. After a season of deep despair, he made another stab at politics. This time he finally won a congressional seat, only to lose his bid for reelection. When he limped home from Washington D.C., he applied for a job as a land officer in his home state—only to be turned down as overqualified.

Five years later, he ran for the U.S. Senate and lost. Sympathetic colleagues nominated him for Vice President at his party's national convention. He only received a handful of votes. Two years later, he picked himself up off the floor and ran again for the U.S. Senate. When he was defeated, he gained the dubious distinction of being one of the biggest losers in the history of American politics.

It staggers the imagination that two years later he somehow found the courage to run for the highest office in the land. In 1860, after decades of repeated failures and personal setbacks, Abraham Lincoln become the 16th President of the United States.

His euphoria was short-lived. As the country careened toward Civil War, he was vilified across the South. Newspapers lampooned him as the "Gorilla from Illinois." When the Union dissolved, there were calls for his impeachment. His generals refused to obey his orders. Members of his cabinet plotted against him. His eleven year-old son died in the White House, and his wife roamed the halls crazy with grief. Given his tragic life, it seems almost fitting that he should have been denied the pleasure of savoring his greatest triumph when he was assassinated at Ford's Theater only six days after the Civil War ended in victory for the Union.

When they emptied the pockets of his bloodstained coat, they found a worn newspaper clipping. It reported a speech by John Bright who called Lincoln "one of the greatest men of all time." The clipping was falling apart from being folded and unfolded so many times. There is something pathetically poignant about this president finding comfort by daily reading and rereading praise from a British politician during those dark years when his own nation ridiculed him."

Standing by Lincoln's deathbed, Secretary of War Edwin Stanton whispered, "Now he belongs to the ages." Two days after his death on Good Friday, preachers eulogized him as the savior of his nation on Easter Sunday. As the funeral train carried his body to its final resting place, millions gathered to weep along the route. Today, he is revered as America's greatest leader. His dogged determination proved that line from Tolstoy: "The two most powerful warriors are patience and time."

When a younger Lincoln was asked the secret to his perseverance, he responded, "I keep preparing in the hopes that someday my chance will come." Before Moses was ready to lead, he had to spend forty years on the Sinai. Desert crossings use patience and time to transform God's people. In the desert of waiting, hold on to this principle:

GOD'S TIME IS NOT ALWAYS OUR TIME, BUT IT IS ALWAYS THE RIGHT TIME.

Are you discouraged today? Maybe you have waited for your finances to improve, an illness to go away, or a marriage to improve. Only you and your Creator know the things that test your patience. Waiting on God may be the hardest of all spiritual disciplines. Humorist Barbara Johnson says, "Patience is the ability to idle your motor when you are stripping your gears." Exodus has five truths for those who don't want to strip their gears.

1. TRANSFORMATION TAKES TIME

Just before St. Stephen was martyred, he preached a sermon about Moses to his killers. He filled in some details that are left out of the Exodus narrative:

> "...Pharaoh's daughter took him and brought him up as her own son. Moses was educated in all the wisdom of the Egyptians and was powerful in speech and actions."
>
> *Acts 7:20&21*

When he appears in the second chapter of Exodus, Moses is forty years old. The Prince of Egypt is razor sharp, Grade "A" steel. He walks with a swagger and speaks with authority. But he is not yet ready for prime time. Moses' outward swagger marks an inner schizophrenia. There are two people battling within this conflicted prince.

ABRAHAM IN MOSES

God orchestrated the rescue of a Jewish baby from a pharaoh's genocide by letting the basket carrying Moses float into the bathing pool of a sympathetic Egyptian princess. He arranged circumstances so that the baby's slave mother could become his wet nurse. Each day that nameless woman not only gave the growing boy her milk, she also fed him her faith. She told her son about the God of the Israelites and the covenant he made with Abraham. In those years before he was weaned, his birth mother gave Moses his identity as a child of Abraham's covenant. That's the key to what happens later:

> "One day after Moses had grown up, he went out to where
> his own people were and watched them at hard labor. He
> saw an Egyptian beating a Hebrew, one of his own people."
>
> *Exodus 2:11*

In Acts 7:25, Stephen says that Moses purposely went out there to rescue his people. He believed that God had placed him strategically to liberate them. When Exodus 2:11 says that he "watched them at their hard labor," the Hebrew language has the sense that he was carefully studying the situation and formulating a plan.

Maybe, when she was catechizing her little Moses, his Jewish mother told him about a prophecy that God had given Abraham some 500 years earlier in the 15th chapter of Genesis: his descendants would be slaves in a strange country and abused for 400 years. But they would come out of this land of slavery with great possessions, and afterwards seize their Promised Land.

Moses did the math. When he was forty years old it had been

almost 400 years since the twelve great-grandsons of Abraham settled in Egypt. He must have reasoned that it was time for God's prophecy to be fulfilled, and that Providence had placed him in the perfect position to get the ball rolling.

It took courage and faith for Moses to walk away from the privileges and pleasures of a palace to throw his lot in with slaves. This decision is celebrated in Hebrews 11:24-26.

> "By faith Moses, when he had grown up, refused to be known as the son of Pharaoh's daughter. He chose to be mistreated along with the people of God rather than to enjoy the pleasures of sin for a short time. He regarded disgrace for the sake of Christ as of greater value than the treasures of Egypt because he was looking ahead to his reward."

Stand in awe of this decision. Moses had the potential to sit on the throne of the greatest superpower on planet earth. But he was gripped by a bigger vision given to him by a nameless slave woman years before. It was the same dream God had given Abraham: that a great Son would come from his lineage. This Son would bless the whole world, bringing salvation to people from every tongue, tribe, and nation until the descendants of that old patriarch were as numerous as the stars in the heavens.

We know that this son was none other than Jesus Christ. His resurrected majesty eclipses the god-kings of Egypt whose mummies rot beneath the sands of North Africa. His Kingdom dwarfs the ancient dynasties of the pharaohs in size, duration, and power. Moses understood what missionary Jim Elliott wrote in his diary before his martyrdom:

"He is no fool who gives up what he cannot keep to gain that which he cannot lose."

Some 3400 years ago Moses did not know Jesus Christ with the clarity that we know him today. But he knew enough to walk away from the temporary pleasures of Egypt, even if it meant suffering disgrace with Christ. In that sense, Moses was a far better person than most of us. He was truly a son of Abraham when he walked away from that palace for the last time.

His story should encourage every parent and grandparent. That slave woman had only a few minutes with her son each day for maybe 5-7 years. It wasn't much compared to the forty years that Pharaoh had to craft him in the palace. But she didn't waste a single moment of her precious time. When Moses left his infancy and walked away from his mother for the last time, his faith was set.

No matter how much time you have with your children, they will end up in Pharaoh's clutches—whether it's in the public schools, or university, or a thousand other places that will attempt to seduce them. But take heart! Godly instruction, when your children are babies, is more powerful than anything they will hear in the courts of Egypt. Abraham Lincoln's mother died when he was seven years old, but during the dark years of the Civil War he often said "My mother's prayers have always followed me. They have clung to me all my life."

THE PHARAOH IN MOSES

Moses may have been a son of Abraham, but he was also the adopted grandson of a Pharaoh. Even if our faith is set as children, our original sin nature is further corrupted in the courts of Egypt. Two men wrestle for the soul of Moses: Abraham and Pharaoh.

The faith of Abraham drives him to liberate his people. The influence of Pharaoh causes him to go about it in the wrong way. We read, "Glancing this way and that and seeing no one, he killed the Egyptian and hid him in the sand." (Exodus 2:12) Any righteous person would try to stop a slave driver who is beating a man half to death. That's the Abraham in Moses.

Yet it's the Pharaoh in Moses who acts. When you read that Moses "glanced this way and that" to make sure the coast was clear, you might recall the earlier words of Pharaoh: "The Israelites have become too numerous for us. We must deal shrewdly with them..." (Exodus 1:9&10) The Hebrew word shrewdly means to calculate carefully and act with cunning. That's what Moses did when he made sure that no one was looking and then buried the evidence of his murder in the sand. Moses learned well from the shrewdness of his adopted grandfather. When you read, "...he killed the Egyptian..." you see the murderous heart of a pharaoh who ordered the genocide of Jewish boys.

Moses may have possessed the faith of his Jewish mother, but he played by the rules of his Egyptian grandfather. It's possible to try to achieve godly ends in ungodly ways. Christians do it all the time. I Peter 5:6 says, "Humble yourself under the mighty hand of God that he may lift you up in due time." Moses is anything but humble at this point in his life. He is unwilling to wait on God's timing. So he jumps the gun forty years too soon. He depends on his own strength and shrewdness, and falls flat on his face.

UNIFYING A HEART

The half-brother of Jesus wrote in James 1:8, "...a double-minded man is unstable in all his ways." The original Greek could be translated, "a man with two souls..." Moses is a combination of Abraham and Pharaoh. As you can see in Exodus two, that makes him very unstable. Others see his "double soul." The next day, when he comes out to kick-start the Jewish liberation movement, one of the slaves responds,

"Who made you ruler and judge over us? Are you thinking of killing me the way you killed the Egyptian."

Exodus 2:14

He is saying in effect, "We saw the way you operated yesterday. It was just like a pharaoh. Why should we exchange an Egyptian murderer for a Jewish murderer?" On the other hand, we read in verse fifteen, "When Pharaoh heard of this, he tried to kill Moses." Remember, this pharaoh is shrewd. He now knows that forty years in the palace haven't exorcised the Abraham in his adopted grandson. Instead, the palace has crafted a skillful revolutionary who now poses a clear and present danger to his throne.

Because Moses is both Abraham and Pharaoh, he is neither. The Jews won't follow him because of the pharaoh in him, and the Pharaoh can't trust him because of the Jew in him. People won't entrust their lives to people who aren't centered. That's why Moses had to wait forty more years. Exodus 2:16 says, "But Moses fled from Pharaoh and went to live in Midian." Like Abraham Lincoln and the rest of us, he had to cross the desert of failure and loneliness. He was forced to stay there until he became a single, unified, godly person. Transformation always takes time.

2. PATIENCE REWARDS TIME

Again, Tolstoy's words: "The two most powerful warriors

are patience and time." Time develops patience, and patience rewards time. They always work in tandem. It couldn't have been easy for the Prince of Egypt to spend the next forty years on the backside of a desert. He who commanded men now herds sheep. The man who dined with kings now travels among nomads. Exodus 2:23 says of those years, "The Israelites groaned in their slavery and cried out..." The clock is ticking, but God will wait until Moses is eighty years old, his skills have rusted and his strength has diminished.

God is frustratingly slow. He sits calmly on his throne while our dreams dissipate. But God doesn't waste a moment. Every second of transformation is prime time. When someone asked Abraham Lincoln if he thought all his years of failure were wasted years, he replied, "In the end, it's not the years in your life that count, but the life in your years." Patience is the ability to let the desert do its work, no matter how long it takes.

3. THE ISSUE IS GOD'S GLORY, NOT OUR PLEASURE

Sin's deception is so subtle. Hebrews 11:25 says that Moses walked away from "the pleasures" of Pharaoh's palace. But he didn't walk away from the pleasures of pride. He still wanted to do God's work in his own way, according to his own timetable. Sometimes there is more sin in God's house than in Pharaoh's palace. It is worse for the fact that it hides behind the "god" language of self-serving purveyors of piety.

During the Civil War both Southerners and Yankees said that theirs was a holy cause. When asked whose side God was on, President Lincoln replied, "Sir, my concern is not whether God is on our side, but whether we are on his side—for God alone is right." Moses thought that he was on God's side when he killed the Egyptian. He would have been shocked if someone said that he was doing the devil's work. We children of Abraham would be shocked if we only knew how much of "God's work" we do in the devil's way. Nothing less than a season on the desert can teach us how to discern the difference between what we do for our own pleasure and what is done for God's glory.

4. USEFULNESS IS SHAPED IN THE DESERT, NOT THE PALACE

At age forty, the Prince of Egypt saw leadership as an exercise of power. That's how princes everywhere, from the banks of the Nile to the banks of the Potomac to the banks on Wall Street, see leadership. No wonder Egypt is now a country where tourists visit the ruins of failed pharaohs. Will busloads of tourists come someday to see the ruined capitals of failed postmodern politicians and the fallen temples of failed preachers?

Greatness is not forged at Harvard, West Point, or even at Evangelical Seminaries. It is found on deserts where an eighty year old failed prince sees the glory of God in a burning bush and cries out in Exodus 3:11, "Who am I that I should go to Pharaoh?" In short, "Who am I that I should dare do the work of the Great I AM?" For the rest of his life this man, who is transformed in the desert of tribulation, will not make a move without saying, "We will not go unless your Presence goes with us." (Exodus 33:15)

The palace creates people without hearts. The desert strips us of our pretense and reduces us to dependence on God's heart. If you want to be useful to God and others, you will "count it all joy" when you are called to the desert crossing.

5. THERE ARE NO WASTED MOMENTS

Moses surely thought the prime of his life had been wasted on the Sinai. Forty years dulled his "palace" edge. But in the Sinai he learned how to lead sheep across a wilderness. He needed that training because he would lead 3.6 million cantankerous Israeli sheep across that same desert. At the end of those "wasted" years he knew the Sinai like the back of his hand: every star in the desert skies, every water hole, the patterns of the seasons, the migrations of the desert tribes, and every inch of the most desolate moonscape on planet earth.

Remember, God's time is not our time, but it's always the right time. We cry out, "Enough already!" We want the desert crossing to end, thinking that we have learned all we need to know. But we don't yet know all there is to know.

Only God knows the beginning from the end. He will not keep us on the desert a second longer than necessary. Neither will he take us off a second earlier than needed. We will know that we are being transformed when we can relax in his timing, and sing with gusto the words of that old hymn, "What ere my God ordains is right."

DESERT REFLECTIONS

Like Moses, your impatience and imprudence may have put you on a desert of your own making. But even our sins and stupidities become tools in God's hands. Our Lord specializes in using our worst failures to transform us into his glorious likeness. If you are on the desert, remember that time and patience are allies of your transformation.

Where would America be today if Abraham Lincoln hadn't persevered through his desert years? Surely, his years in the wilderness were preparing him to lead his divided nation through the wilderness years of the Civil War. If you will take the time to study the greatest leaders in history, you will discover that every one of them went through prolonged desert crossings.

Winston Churchill labored in obscurity and loneliness most of his adult life before he was plucked from obscurity to lead England through her darkest years. He later said, "All of my successes have been built on a solid foundation of failures." Like Lincoln, Moses, and so many others, Churchill led his people across the same desert that he had crossed for so many years. And so will you, if you will patiently wait on God's perfect timing.

Don't you dare give up on one of the great doctrines of the Scriptures: the perseverance of the saints. Just keep your eyes on Jesus who persevered to the end in order to glorify his Father in heaven. Remember, he who finished his race is also the "author and finisher" of your race too. (Hebrews 12:2)

WEAKNESS

DESERT 3

"I feel like a solitary bird warbling his little song against the wind, but no one hears."

Martin Luther

It was the social event of the season. Men in tuxedos and women in evening gowns had packed Carnegie Hall to hear the Polish composer and pianist, Jan Paderewski.

In the hall that evening was a little boy who wished that he could be anywhere in the world but this concert. But his mother had dragged him there in the hope that, if he saw Paderewski perform, he might be inspired to practice his piano more diligently.

As his mother visited with friends before the concert began, the boy slipped down the row, and then up the aisle, drawn by the ebony Steinway Grand on the stage. Looking both ways, he climbed onto the platform, sat down at the piano, placed trembling fingers on the keyboard and began to play... Chopsticks.

A hush fell over the hall. Then that well-heeled audience of sophisticates turned into a screaming mob.

> "Who let that kid up on the stage?"
> "Someone get that brat away from the piano!"
> "Where's that boy's mother?"
> "Hey, kid, get off the stage!"

Paralyzed by fear, he continued to play Chopsticks over and over again. Upon hearing the uproar back stage, Paderewski rushed to the edge of the curtain where he saw the terrified boy confronted by the snarling mob. The maestro strode across the stage, circled his arms around the boy, and began to improvise a countermelody to harmonize with and enhance Chopsticks. All the time he kept whispering in the boy's ear, "Don't stop now. Whatever else you do kid, keep on playing. Keep on playing."

Do you ever feel like that boy? It seems like the whole world is yelling, "Hey, kid, get off the stage!" And all you can manage on the stage of life is to play Chopsticks?

Surely Moses felt that way. At age forty this adopted Prince of Egypt was at the peak of his prime. He was sharpened to a razor's edge and polished to perfection—a sword of war, resting in the hand of a Pharaoh who shaped him to expand an empire. But he turned against the god-king and tried to spark a slave rebellion. His mettle cracked under the stress and shattered. He ended up a fugitive on the run, hiding out in the most desolate badlands on planet earth. And the passing years turned a prince's swagger into an old man's limp.

Long ago, he buried his dreams in the graveyard of broken hearts. Then God showed up unexpectedly, speaking out of a burning bush and telling Moses that it was time for him to go back to Egypt and free his people. Why does God come to him now when the skills of the palace and the strength of his youth have long ago dissipated? If he couldn't liberate his people when he was in the peak of his prime, how can he do it now? All of us who have been dissipated by the desert can take hope in this principle:

GOD'S STRENGTH IS MADE PERFECT IN OUR WEAKNESS.

Moses protested in Exodus 3:11, "Who am I that I should go to Pharaoh and bring the Israelites out of Egypt?" Do you hear the silent scream from the old man's soul: "Please don't make me dig up the bones of my failed dreams, lest I suffer disappointment again!" Like Moses, we often bury our dreams to protect our hearts.

Perhaps you are feeling the inadequacy of Moses. Maybe physical ailments, emotional struggles, or moral failures have sapped your resolve. Or you are on the ragged edge of giving up on your marriage, children, or church. Only you and God know the places where the desert has eroded your soul.

Moses needs to discover that shattered and rusted steel is infinitely more useful in God's hand than the strongest "palace" steel in a pharaoh's hand. After he wrestled with his "thorn in the flesh" for years, St. Paul heard God say, "My power is made perfect in weakness." (2 Corinthians 12:9) For all of us who need some steel in our soul, here are three transforming truths:

1. IT'S NOT WHAT WE ARE, BUT WHO GOD IS

When God told this eighty-year-old bundle of insecurities to go down and confront Pharaoh, he responded with two questions in the 3rd Chapter of Exodus.

"WHO AM I?"

In Exodus 3:11 he gave his first reply: "Who am I that I should go to Pharaoh and bring the Israelites out of Egypt?" This is always the wrong question because the issue is never who we are. Moses calculated his chances by focusing on himself. If Moses had posed the same question at age forty, he would have responded, "I'm somebody. As the Prince of Egypt I possess everything I need to liberate my people." He was self-confident, self-assertive, and self-motivated. Most of us would applaud Moses for his good self-image at age forty. But the confident prince imploded like a house of cards.

At age eighty, Moses answered the question far differently: "I'm nobody. Just a stuttering old shepherd. If I ever had the right stuff, I don't anymore!" Now he has a deflated self-esteem. He's self-loathing, self-condemning, and self-deprecating. But self-pity is no better. It's just the other side of the coin of self-pride.

When we see people who are down on themselves, we often blurt out, "If only they had a better self-image or more self-esteem." But, that is precisely the problem. Whether people struggle with self-pity or self-pride, the root is the same: self. Expand self and you get the word selfish. God's people would do better if they would exorcise those words, self-image and self-esteem, from their lexicons and replace them with words like God-image or Christ-esteem. "Who am I?" is always the wrong question because it always focuses on the wrong person.

"WHO ARE YOU, GOD?"

If Moses is going to get off his desert of despair he needs to take the focus off himself. His second question makes all the difference in the world:

> "Suppose I go to the Israelites and say to them, 'The God of your fathers has sent me to you; and they ask me, 'What is his name?' Then what shall I say to them?"
>
> *Exodus 3:13*

The issue is not what we are, but who God is. God answers the old man, "I AM WHO I AM. This is what you are to say to the Israelites, 'I AM has sent me to you." (Exodus 3:14) The Jewish rabbis say that there are 7,000 names for God. But in verse fifteen, God says that I AM is his most important name. What a strange name—I AM. Let's allow some well-known theologians to share insights on the richness of this name.

I REALLY AM

The great theologian and apologist Francis Schaeffer would tell you that I AM is God's way of saying that he is or he exists. In his book *The God Who is There*, Schaeffer says that the two fundamental facts of Judeo-Christianity are established in the 3rd chapter of Exodus: 1) God is, and 2) He is not silent.

But sometimes God is silent. Exodus 2:23 says that, during Moses' long exile on the Sinai, "...the Israelites groaned in their slavery and cried out..." Archeologists have found a short but agonizing prayer written in ancient Hebrew graffiti on the walls of a cave in Egypt: "Help me God!" But for forty years this desperate prayer was mocked by heaven's silence.

In his book *A Grief Observed,* C.S. Lewis writes a heart wrenching account of his own desert crossing after his wife died of cancer. He complained of desperate prayers greeted by mocking silence. The silence of heaven made Lewis doubt if God really cared, or even existed anymore. But the fact that God doesn't speak is not proof that he doesn't see or hear. He says to Moses, "I have indeed seen the misery of my people in Egypt. I have heard them crying out because of their slave drivers." (Exodus 3:7) And, the fact that God is silent doesn't mean that he doesn't care. He goes on in Exodus 3:7 to say, "...and I am concerned about their suffering." When we are going through our deepest pain, the person who sits silently by our side is the one who cares most and comforts most.

Our media-saturated age abhors silence. Our senses are bombarded with images, music and messages around the clock. In a culture that leaves no room for silence, God's people need to remember his plea: "Be still and know that I AM God." (Psalm 46:10) Rather than seeing silence as a proof that God doesn't exist, we should see it as the place where we can find him.

When God is silent, it may be that he's waiting for us to stop talking. Or he's just waiting quietly for the right time to speak or act. He says to Moses in Exodus 3:8, "So I have come down to rescue them from the land of the Egyptians and to bring them up out of the land into a good and spacious land."

I AM WHO I AM, NOT WHO YOU WISH I WAS

Theologian R.C. Sproul adds another take on the name I AM. He says that God is saying, "I am who I am, not what you think me to be, or imagine me to be, or want me to be, or wish me to be, or make me to be." The great I AM will not allow us to give him a makeover. He is unchangeable. Later, at Mt. Sinai, the Israelites will attempt to change the unchangeable God into a little golden bull. There is nothing more dehumanizing than idolatry. The gods of our creation can never be bigger than our finite imaginations. But the God of Abraham, Isaac, and Jacob is the great I AM—infinitely bigger than our cosmos, more than sufficient to break our chains and get us to our Promised Land.

THE EVER-PRESENT NOW

A.W. Tozer adds something else about the I AM in his classic book *Knowledge of the Holy*. He reminds us that I AM is a present tense verb in the Hebrew language. God is saying that he lives in the ever-present now. A never-ending song before the throne of God declares, "Holy, holy, holy is the Lord Almighty who was, and is, and is to come." (Revelation 4:8) Hebrews 13:8 says that Jesus is God because he is "...the same yesterday, today, and forever." Tozer says that the I AM is the God of the past, the present, and the future—at the same time. There's never a moment he isn't there for us.

THE I AM OF PSALM 23

No one described the great I AM better than David in the 23rd Psalm. He says, "He leads me beside still waters." (verse two) If he leads me, that means he goes ahead of me, and will be where I am going before I get there. In short, he is already in my future while I am still in my present. Tomorrow Moses is going to the Egyptian palace to face the most powerful man on earth. If he thinks about all the dangers in his future, he can be paralyzed with fear. But I AM wants Moses to know that, though he

and even use it as a weapon to ward off predators. God must be saying to Moses,

"You are like this crooked old stick. You weren't much when I found you on the desert. But I've decided to pick you up and use you. You're now my stick. I'm going to lean on you, and use you to prod my sheep all the way to the Promised Land and fight off predators who try to harm them."

But it's hard to convince a crooked stick that it can be useful in God's hand. So he commands Moses in Exodus 4:3, "Throw the stick on the ground." It turns into a snake. It must be a dangerous serpent because Moses runs from it. God is showing Moses that when the Holy Spirit invades a stick, it becomes deadly. God hasn't called us to be nice, safe religious folk. He is looking for dangerous Christians who will take a bite out of this corrupt and compassionless world.

But most of us are as afraid of the snake in the stick as we are of the fire in the bush. Spirit-filled Christianity is never for the faint of heart. So God commands Moses in Exodus 4:4, "Reach out your hand and take hold of it by the tail." Anyone who has ever handled a snake knows that the most dangerous place to grab it is by its tail. The moment you do, the snake will spin around and bite you. This is God's way of saying to Moses, "Don't run from the power of the Holy Spirit. You can handle it." Later this stick will become very dangerous. As it is held up, rivers will turn to blood, plagues will strike the land, and the Red Sea will come crashing down on Pharaoh's grand army.

The magicians at Pharaoh's court also had sticks. Theirs were slick sticks, varnished to a high gloss and adorned with silver and gold. They could turn their slick sticks into snakes by a magician's slight of hand. Moses' old stick looked unimpressive up against these slick sticks. But, when Moses stood in the

Pharaoh's throne room, the snake in his old stick slithered across the floor and gobbled up the snakes that came from slick sticks. There are lots of slick sticks in this world: slick stick politicians, slick stick celebrities, and even slick stick preachers. But God prefers old desert sticks to the slick sticks of the palace. Nothing is more powerful than the crooked stick on which Jesus was crucified, unless it is a crooked stick saint filled with his resurrected power and presence.

A SHAKING HAND FILLED WITH LIFE AND DEATH

Moses is still unconvinced. So, in Exodus 4:6 God tells the old man to look at his hand. My father was a big fisherman with massive hands. When I was a teenager, we often arm-wrestled. I couldn't budge those muscular arms and gigantic hands that hauled in nets full of king salmon. I'll never forget a day when he was 85 years old. We had stopped for hamburgers at a fast food place, and he was trying to open one of those cellophane ketchup packets. But he wasn't strong enough. I looked at his shaking hands, lined with blue veins and splotched with age spots. I wanted to cry. As I helped him rip open the ketchup wrapper, I wondered if Moses' hands were as weak as his.

You can almost hear Moses say, "My hands are too weak for the job." So God says, in Exodus 4:6, "Put your hand in the cloak." The hand becomes leprous. When Moses sees it he is as frightened as when he saw the fire in the bush and the snake in the stick. He puts his hand back into his cloak, and it comes out restored—as soft as a newborn baby's skin. God is giving a third picture: when his Holy Spirit possesses a hand it has the power of life and death; leprosy and birth; healing and plague; blessings and curses. All of these things and more will take place when Moses stretches forth his hand.

In God's hand, even the weakest hands are strong. More than that, God's strength is actually made perfect in our weakness. It doesn't matter what we are because everything hinges on who God is. It doesn't matter where we are, but where we are going. It doesn't even matter what's on the outside as long as Jesus is on the inside. When that happens, old bushes catch on fire; crooked sticks become snakes; and shaking hands change the world.

DESERT REFLECTIONS

Deserts are designed to reduce you to weakness. The continued onslaughts of the desert crossing erode your self-confidence until you are forced to put your confidence in the great I AM. But beware of a subtle trap in the desert crossing: like Moses, you can turn it into your desert hideaway. Having experienced past failures and defeats, you might be afraid to go back and risk another disappointment.

But the desert of tribulation is a transitory crossing, not a terminal location. God's design is that you eventually come out of the desert for three reasons: 1) to lead those who are enslaved in Egypt to freedom in Christ; 2) to help others make it across deserts that you have already learned how to cross; and 3) to move on to your Promised Land that is beyond deserts yet to cross.

Yet right now the crowd is screaming, "Get off the stage, kid!" Paralyzed by fear, you fumble through your Chopsticks. Please, stop and listen. Do you hear the Master coming softly on sandaled feet? Can you feel his arms encircling you? Do you see his nail-scared hands resting on the keys beside your trembling fingers. Can you hear him turning your Chopsticks into a symphony that was arranged for you before time began? Take heart. It will make the whole world sing. Listen to the Master. He is whispering in your ear, "Don't stop now. What ever else you do kid, don't stop playing."

he was forced to reevaluate everything. But even at age eighty, he deceived himself by underestimating his capacity. "O Lord, I have never been eloquent..." Like most of us, he still had more self-deception to be pruned.

A dear friend was recently released from prison. Family and friends rejected him after he committed his felony. Then he was rejected by society and locked away. But in that desert of loneliness, God stripped away years of self-deception. It was a brutal and bleak process. Yet he comes out a purged man who knows his sins, understands grace, and realizes his need to cling to Christ.

If you are crossing the desert of rejection, you too have an opportunity for self-inventory. It doesn't matter if the things said to you were false, or mean-spirited, or even unfair. If you will stop nursing your hurt feelings long enough to let God expose your defects, that rejection will become a scalpel to cut away that which keeps you from being all that Christ redeemed you to become. You can take heart in two facts while you are going through the pain of self-inventory.

GOD WILL NEVER MAKE YOU STAND ALONE

Moses is desperate when he pleads, "O Lord, please send someone else to do it." (Exodus 4:13) God is getting impatient and even angry at Moses' excuses. But he also understands human frailty. He knows that he's not calling Moses to an easy thing. Prophets are never popular. We build monuments to prophets with the same rocks we used to stone them to death. It's deadly dangerous to walk and talk the truth. So, in his tender mercy, God asks,

"What about your brother, Aaron the Levite. I know he can

speak well. He is already on his way to meet you, and his
heart will be glad to see you."

Exodus 4:14

After forty years, Moses is going to be reunited with his
brother. Where he feels weakest, this brother is strongest. Each
of us needs an Aaron to watch our back. When my friend was in
prison, God gave him Christian brothers. Now that he's facing
life after prison, his church family is standing with him. We can
stand against the world if Aaron stands with us. Every one of
us needs a good friend to walk with us as we cross our deserts.
We need to be a participating member of a good local church. We
need to belong to a small group that will stand with us. No one is
strong enough to go it alone.

At the same time, we must be realistic: Aaron will let us down.
Later, Aaron crafts the golden calf. After that, he teams up with
Moses' sister to oppose his leadership. Our most painful rejection will come from brothers and sisters in the family of God. Yet
Proverbs 19:23 says, "...There is a friend who sticks closer than
a brother." Even when our brothers and sisters reject us, there
is a friend who knows our anguish. He too was rejected by the
people of God. That's why Hebrews 4:13 says of Jesus, "For we
do not have a high priest who is unable to sympathize with our
weakness..." That's also why Hebrews 4:16 can promise, "Let us
then approach the throne of grace with confidence, so that we
may receive mercy and find grace to help in the time of need."
Jesus, the friend who sticks closer than a brother, will never let
us stand alone.

GOD WILL NEVER MAKE YOU STAND WHEN YOU CAN'T

We can only stand so much rejection. Even Jesus came

to the end of himself when he cried out from the cross, "My God, My God, why have you forsaken me?" (Matthew 27:46) God knows how much we are able to bear. He says to Moses in Exodus 4:19, "Go back to Egypt, for all the men who wanted to kill you are dead." Before it's over, there will be a new crop of folks who want to kill Moses. But, at least for now, God is buying him time to do what he has to do.

Our Lord never calls us to do something at the wrong time. That's why we have to wait on him, even if it takes forty years. Yet God will never call us to do something that is beyond our capacity. He will never call us into a battle without arming us. He will never send us across a desert without giving us the necessary food and water. Where he gives a vision, he supplies provision.

There are days when God's call tests every molecule of our body and soul. During those times, cling tenaciously to St. Paul's promise in I Corinthians 10:13:

"No temptation has seized you except what is common to man. And God is faithful; he will not let you be tempted beyond what you can bear. But when you are tempted, he will also provide a way out so that you can stand up under it."

As we grow up in Christ, we need to remember that there really is life after rejection. It might even be helpful to take the humorous approach of author Louise Brown: "I could write an entertaining novel about all the rejection slips I've received, but I fear it would be overly long." But, to turn rejection into a helpful tool for self-inventory, we need to seize a second truth:

2. DON'T GIVE UP UNTIL THE INVENTORY IS COMPLETED

Rejection is God's discipline. Hebrews 12:11 says, "No discipline seems pleasant at the time..." You will be tempted to avoid rejection at all costs, even if it means compromising your faith. If you are facing it right now, you probably want to run away like Moses and hide in some desert. But if you refuse to flinch in the face of this discipline, Hebrews 12:11 says, "...Later on it produces a harvest of righteousness and peace." Hebrews 12:12 concludes, "Therefore, strengthen your feeble arms and weak knees..."

Discipline is a gradual process, like crossing a long desert. We need to hang in to the end, letting the discipline of God finish its good work. So, when we feel like giving up, we need to strengthen ourselves with these facts:

REJECTION BY PHARAOHS IS NOT PERSONAL

In Egypt, his slave family gives Moses a hero's welcome. They are overjoyed that God heard their prayers. But happy revival turns to harsh reality. Moses stands before the god-king of Egypt to deliver a command from his God that can be reduced to four words in Exodus 5:1: "Let my people go!" The god-king responds,

"Who is the LORD that I should obey him and let Israel go?
I do not know the LORD; and I will not let Israel go."
Exodus 5:2

Moses could take this rejection as personal. But this isn't his battle. He's just the ringside announcer for a super heavyweight battle:

"Ladies and gentlemen, in this corner is the great I AM. In the other corner, introducing the king of Egypt. He is a god on earth, worshipped by his subjects, his glory inscribed on pyramids, and his person backed by the greatest empire in history! Now, let's get ready to rumble!"

This epic fight will be a power encounter between the great I AM and the pretender god of Egypt. The great I AM will clobber this god-king with ten rounds of plagues. His armies will go down for the count, and Egypt will never recover her former glory.

If the people of this world reject us, it's not personal. They are rejecting the God in us. If they hated Jesus, they will hate us. Like Pharaoh, they joke that our God is the creation of uneducated, unscientific fundamentalism. Non-believing relatives dismiss our values as judgmental and narrow-minded. Let me repeat: it's not personal. But it will expose our pride and bring out the worst in us. That's okay. God is using the Egyptians to purge our sin. The more our faith is attacked, the better it will become.

REJECTION BY GOD'S PEOPLE IS PERFECTING

In the first round of this super-heavyweight fight, the god-king lands a vicious uppercut. He loads even more work on the Jewish slaves. Instead of freedom, Moses has made their bondage worse. In Exodus 5:20 the Israelites lash out at Moses, "May the Lord look upon you and judge you! You have made us a stench to Pharaoh and his officials and have put a sword in their hand to kill us."

To be attacked by God's people is the cruelest blow of all. When rejection comes lathered with god-talk, it's even worse:

"May the Lord look upon you and judge you!" Every pastor will tell you that the most ungodly rejection comes wrapped in the most sanctimonious language from the most pious people. Even Jesus was taken aback when Judas betrayed him with a kiss. God's people can be unspeakably cruel. They are even capable of crucifying their Savior.

Rejection also brings perfection. At age forty, Moses murdered a man in a fit of anger. At age eighty, when he saw God's people worshipping the golden calf, he exploded in anger and smashed the Stone Tablets of the Law to smithereens. At age eighty-five, when God's people complained about a lack of water, he smacked the rock instead of speaking to it as the Lord commanded. That outburst of anger kept him out of the Promised Land.

But, eventually Moses overcame his abiding sin. Toward the end of his life, God could say in Numbers 12:3, "Now Moses was a very humble man, more humble than anyone else on the face of the earth."

Even the most painful rejection by God's people perfects us. Joseph's brothers sold him into Egyptian slavery. For the next twelve years Joseph experienced one rejection after another. But those rejections perfected Joseph and set in motion a chain of events that put him in a position to save his people from a famine. When his brothers stood before him, Joseph was the Prime Minister of Egypt, with the power to exact retribution. Instead he said in Genesis 50:20: "You intended to harm me, but God intended it for good." Joseph saw their rejection as a tool used by God to transform him so that he could be in a position to transform others.

REJECTING GOD REVEALS THE PHARAOH STILL IN US

Rejection runs downhill. The Pharaoh rejects God and oppresses God's people even more. God's people respond by rejecting Moses. Moses reacts by lashing out at God,

> "O Lord why have you brought trouble upon this people?
> Is this why you sent me? Ever since I went to Pharaoh
> to speak in your name, he has brought trouble upon this
> people, and you have not rescued your people at all."
>
> *Exodus 5:22&23*

Isn't it fascinating how everything goes full circle? Pharaoh scorns God; God's people scorn Moses; and Moses scorns God. In the end, the Pharaoh and the Prophet both question the will of God. Remember what we learned earlier: Moses possessed the faith of Abraham given by his mother. But he also thought like his adopted pharaoh grandfather. Like Moses, we all have too much Egypt in us. We think we know better than God. That's why we still need to be pruned by rejection.

AVOID REJECTION BY GOD AT ALL COSTS

There is a rejection we should fear most. Let's look at a frightening moment when Moses was going back to Egypt from the Sinai. Exodus 4:24, says that the LORD came after Moses to kill him. How strange! God has called Moses to go to Egypt to free his people. And now he is going to kill him, because he neglected to circumcise his son?

Why is that such a big deal? Circumcision is the sign of God's covenant with Abraham that promises the Savior of the world. God has commanded all descendants of Abraham to put the sign of the covenant on their children. To forget that, is to disobey God. By forgetting to circumcise his son, Moses was saying that the covenant of grace was unimportant. In a way he was denying the Christ who was yet to come.

It is a fearful thing to fall into the hands of a living God. But Moses' wife Zipporah quickly circumcised their firstborn son and put the boy's bloody foreskin on his feet. Exodus 4:16 says, "So the Lord let him alone." What saves us from God's rejection? The Gospel of Christ is our only hope. You see it pre-figured here. The blood of Zipporah's son covers Moses. In the same way, Mary's firstborn son Jesus was cut at the cross so that his blood would cover those under the death sentence of God.

That gospel will again be prefigured in the last plague on Passover night. The death angel will kill the firstborn sons of Egypt avenging all the Jewish baby boys who have been slaugh-tered by the Egyptians. But the blood of the lamb, sprinkled on the doorposts of Jewish homes, will save them from the wrath of God. Just as the Egyptian god-king's firstborn son is killed, so will I AM's Only Begotten Son be killed on a Roman Cross. His blood is shed so that we could escape the rejection of God, just as Moses did when his firstborn son's blood covered his feet. It is our only hope.

Most of us are consumed by what others feel about us. There are few pains more excruciating than rejection. So we fear people, rather than please God. Instead, we should fear God, rather than please people. At the Final Judgment we will stand stark naked and alone before an all-knowing God and give an account of our lives. On that day it won't matter how many people we have pleased. But our eternity will hang on whether or not we have pleased the great I AM.

The truth is: none of us can perfectly please a perfect God. Even spiritual giants like Moses slip up. But Jesus did perfectly please his heavenly Father. It is only when we put our trust in his perfect righteousness, as the only basis of our salvation, that we can be seen as righteous and perfectly pleasing in God's sight.

DESERT REFLECTIONS

Peter Tchaikovsky was right: "None but the lonely can feel my anguish." Perhaps you wonder if anyone understands the pain and loneliness that you are going through.

Christ knows your anguish. He has experienced it. He knows your pain when you feel rejected by God because of your sins. His heavenly Father forsook him when he took your sins upon himself on the cross.

He knows the anguish you feel when others reject you because of your weakness. When he was on earth, those who were disappointed in him rejected him. He understands your shame when you reject yourself because of the secret sins you carry. He felt the shame of carrying all the secret sins of a world of lost sinners.

Christ loves you so much that he was willing to be forsaken by his Father so that that his Father could accept you. He was rejected by the world so that you would be redeemed from the world.

Indeed, you never stand alone when you stand with the Only Begotten Son of God.

Lord, John Acton famously wrote, "Great men are seldom good men." BoYa 'Lyowb was both great and good; that rarest of persons who is rich and righteous at the same time. His impeccable integrity was the toast of the business world. His legendary wisdom caused top leaders to seek his counsel. When BoYa 'Lyowb walked into a room, everyone stood. When he spoke, they all listened.

Not only did 'Lyowb reach the highest rung of the ladder of success, he earned the applause of heaven. When God peered into the secret places of Mr. 'Lyowb's life, he saw no hypocrisy. He even bragged to the angels that BoYa 'Lyowb's life was blameless.

Maybe that's why, some 4,000 years later, his monumental collapse still causes us to ask, "How could so many bad things happen to such a good person?" In the space of a few days, his financial empire imploded, his children were killed, and he was left an invalid—his body disfigured with reeking, loathsome boils.

By now you might be remembering BoYa 'Lyowb by his more familiar name. BoYa is an ancient Semitic word which means "hated" or "persecuted." It's a name that later Jewish Talmudic writers gave him. The name 'Lyowb is an earlier Jewish version of Jobé, or its later pronunciation: Job.

Most folks think that the storyline of Job is his patience in the light of suffering. But, if you scratch beneath the surface, you will discover that it is more about his integrity. Twice the word "integrity" is used in the opening lines of Job's story. Did you know that this is the first time in literature that the word "integrity" is ever used? It's appropriate that a book written by God should introduce the concept of integrity. God says this about BoYa 'Lyowb when he talks to Satan in Job 2:3: "He still maintains his integrity, though you incited me against him to ruin him without reason."

Later BoYa's wife has an emotional meltdown. After burying ten children, she is forced to watch her husband suffer horrific agony. She endures this while buried in the ruins of her shattered life. We can sympathize when she lashes out at her husband, "Are you still holding on to your integrity? Curse God and die!" (Job 2:9 NIV)

There's that word integrity again. What does it mean? We get a hint when BoYa responds in Job 2:10, "Shall we accept good from God, and not trouble?" Job is saying that it doesn't matter whether times are good or bad, his faith is still the same. It never changes with the circumstances. Integrity is the inner core of your being that doesn't blow in the wind or change with the weather.

The Hebrew word for integrity in Job's story is powerful. It is used to describe fabric or cloth that is one piece, seamless, without rips or cuts. Integrity means that your life is undivided. Job would say, "You can't have one faith for the good times and a different one for the bad." King David was thinking about integrity when he begged God in Psalm 86:11, "Give me an undivided heart."

What is integrity? Mark Twain wrote, "It is to live in such a way that you will never be afraid to sell your parrot to the town gossip." Job never wavered in his core beliefs about God. He lived by the same faith in his sufferings as he did in his successes. This is critical for all of us who are called to an exodus.

Remember, the road to the Promised Land always leads through the desert. Just as Job's integrity was tested in the bad times, the integrity of those who follow Moses will also be tested. Will their faith be as strong in arid deserts as when water miraculously gushes from rocks? Will it be as strong when they are hungry as when they are gorging on manna and quail? In short, will their walk match their talk? It's so easy to compromise integrity when tough times come.

As the Exodus narrative continues, Moses is caught in the Pharaoh's crosshairs. This god-king of Egypt is the most powerful man on planet earth. And he is dead set against letting 3.6 million Jewish slaves leave Egypt. God responds by sending horrific plagues on the land. They only manage to harden the stubborn resolve of this god-king. And he responds by tempting Moses to compromise his integrity. For those of us who face the same temptation, it's critical that we grasp the fifth principle from Exodus:

THERE ARE NO SHORTCUTS TO THE PROMISED LAND.

All of us have spent time in an Egypt of our own making. Everyone of us has been in bondage to sin. We didn't bow our knee to the Pharaoh, but we served the Devil. Yet, through Jesus' work, we have been taken out of the land of bondage. In the same way those ancient Jews went through the Red Sea, so we went through our own baptism experience. And now we are on the road to possessing all the promises God has for those who follow Christ. But we still struggle with abiding habits, old addictions, emotional hang ups, and attacks by the enemies of our soul. For that reason, we will go through a string of desert experiences so that God can transform and perfect us.

If the devil can't keep us in bondage, then he will discourage us along the way in order to tempt us to go back to Egypt. He will tell the lie that we can have both Egypt and the Promised Land at the same time. His chief tactic will be to offer the easy shortcut of compromise.

Maybe you are barely hanging on today. Your life is fraying at the ragged edges. Your resolve to remain holy in the face of some temptation is starting to rip apart. Perhaps you hear the voice of Job's wife screaming in your soul, "Are you still holding on to your integrity?"

The Hebrew word for "holding on" speaks of desperation. Job is holding on for dear life to his integrity. As the winds of suffering rip at the fabric of his faith, he is fighting to keep his actions from being separated from his core beliefs. Job would agree with former Wyoming Senator Alan Simpson: "If you have integrity, nothing else matters. If you don't have integrity, nothing else matters." Here are four transforming truths from Moses' encounters with Pharaoh that can help you hold on to your integrity:

1. WE HAVE TO LEAVE EGYPT

This contest of wills between a sovereign God and a stubborn god-king is a battle to the death. God repeats the same message: "Let my people go!" The Pharaoh repeats the same response: "No, I won't!" Moses says to the god-king:

> "This is what the Lord, the god of Israel says, 'Let my people go, so that they may hold a festival to me in the desert.'"
>
> *Exodus 5:1*

The Pharaoh wasn't born yesterday. He knows that if 3.6 million Jewish slaves cross the Red Sea and go to the Sinai to worship their God, they aren't coming back. So he refuses to let them go worship. The Devil knows that if we ever begin to worship God, he's lost us. Like the Pharaoh, the Enemy of our soul will pull out all the stops to keep us in bondage. Only God can break the yoke of whatever bondage you are in today.

So God unleashes four ecological disasters: the Nile turns to blood, followed by successive infestations of frogs, gnats, and flies. At that point the Pharaoh offers a shortcut to Moses in Exodus 8:25: "Go, sacrifice to your God here in the land." At first, it seems like a victory for the good guys. "Go, sacrifice to your God..." Religious freedom! It's almost too good to be true. But catch the caveat at the end of verse twenty-five: "...here in the land."

God says, "My people have to leave Egypt before they can worship." Pharaoh answers, "They can worship, but they must do it in Egypt." Do you see the subtle temptation? It is as old as the Garden of Eden. The Serpent says to Adam and Eve, "You can still walk with God while you are eating the forbidden fruit." He comes to us today and says, "You can stay in bondage to your sin and still have fellowship with God." Pharaoh is saying, "You can serve me as your Master and still worship your God." Jesus counters Pharaoh in Matthew 6:24, "No one can serve two masters. Either he will hate the one and love the other, or he will be devoted to the one and despise the other."

Integrity will not allow a divided heart. You can't serve God and money. You can't focus on God while you look at pornography. You can't please God while you are consumed with pleasing people. Bob Dylan used to sing the song, "You've got to serve somebody." But it can only be one somebody.

Moses responds in Exodus 8:26, "That would not be right. The sacrifices we offer the LORD our God would be detestable to the Egyptians..." Moses understands that the enemies of God hate true worship. If we truly live for God, we will be hated. Don't be surprised if the cultural elite dismiss us as narrow-minded Neanderthals who pose a clear and present danger to their progress.

Even if we are gentle, loving, and nonjudgmental in the practice of our Faith, the culture around us will find our worship detestable. We might be tempted to try to make peace by "Egyptianizing" our worship and lifestyle to make it palatable to others. If we do, we will lose our integrity. In The Neurotic Notebook, Mignon McLaughlin gives us a great warning: "It's impossible to be loyal to your family, your country, and your principles all at the same time." It's critical to grasp the fact that we can't get to our Promised Land without cutting ties to Egypt.

2. WE HAVE TO GO ALL THE WAY

When Moses refuses to take the hook, Pharaoh switches the bait. In Exodus 8:28 he says, "I will let you go to offer sacrifices to the Lord your God in the desert, but you must not go very far. Now pray for me." Beware of temptation cloaked in spiritual language. It's the most insidious seduction of all. Even Moses is sucker-punched by Pharaoh's deception. The Egyptian king begins verse 28 by saying, "I will let you go to offer sacrifices to the Lord your God in the desert." It sounds like he is doing everything God commands. He ends Exodus 8:28 by piously saying, "Now pray for me." We might even think that the Pharaoh is softening on the religion of Moses.

But notice the little seduction hidden away in the middle of verse twenty-eight. *"...but you must not go very far..."* This is a lure that snags most postmodern American Christians: we can become followers of Jesus, but we shouldn't take it too far. Pharaoh calls us to a faith without fanaticism. A faith that leaves room for lots of ways to God. A smorgasbord faith where you pick a little of this and a little of that.

The Egyptian Pharaoh masquerades as the religious convert, but he is using the devil's strategies. If the devil loses us to God-worship, he at least wants us to stay close by. But we can't just go ankle deep into faith a few feet from the safety of the shore. Jesus says, "Take up your cross, and die daily..." It's an all or nothing deal. We can't just leave Egypt; we have to go all the way to the Promised Land. This journey comes without a roundtrip ticket.

3. WE HAVE TO TAKE OUR FAMILIES WITH US

After Moses leaves the palace, the Pharaoh's heart is again hardened. We have to give him his due: he doesn't have a divided heart. Sometimes nonbelievers have more integrity in their unbelief than we have in our own belief system. So God pours out four more plagues on Egypt: dead livestock, boils, hailstorms, and locusts. Moses is summoned again. A chastened Pharaoh says in Exodus 10:8, "Go, worship the Lord your God. But who will be going?"

Moses replies in verse nine, "We will go with our young and old, with our sons and daughters, and with our flocks and herds, because we are to celebrate a festival to the Lord." Moses cannot imagine God's people worshipping a covenant-keeping God without their children. Search the Scriptures, and you will never find a single covenant that God makes with his people that doesn't include their children.

But Pharaoh replies in verses Exodus 10:10&11, "...Clearly you are bent on evil. No! Have only the men go, and worship the Lord, since that's what you have been asking for." It's at the point of children and families that Pharaoh becomes most violent. Verse eleven ends, "Then Moses and Aaron were driven out of Pharaoh's presence." The world will not compromise with us when it comes to our children. Pharaoh knows that as long as he holds their families hostage, the men will return.

Satan is still using the same strategy today. He says to us, "You can worship your God as long as you let me have your families. But what have we gained if we worship God on Sunday, and let the Egyptians have our children the rest of the week? We give them over to day care, television, video games, sports, the public schools, the universities, Facebook, text messaging, friends, activities, and a thousand other nannies to shape their lives while we go off to our adult Bible studies and men's groups. Too many Christian men neglect the nurture of their wives and children, while resisting the call to spiritual leadership in their homes.

Moses knows that going to a place of worship without our families is an utter lack of integrity. In postmodern America, 65% of the World War II generation identifies itself as Christians. But that number drops to less than ten percent of those under the age of thirty. We are facing spiritual crisis because our children are growing up as Egyptians. The devil is happy to let the churches fill up with grey hairs as long as he's got the next generation. More than ever, it is imperative that God's people stop at nothing to take their children on their spiritual journey to the Promised Land.

4. WE HAVE TO TAKE OUR POSSESSIONS WITH US

There are no shortcuts. It's all or nothing. God sends a ninth plague, and Egypt plunges into utter darkness. God gives a frightening message to our postmodern generation: if we harden our hearts toward him, our culture will descend into darkness.

Pharaoh plays his last hand: "Go worship the LORD. Even your women and children may go with you; only leave your flocks and herds behind." (Exodus 10:24) This is the ultimate trump card of seduction. We might leave Egypt. We might even commit to heading all the way to the Promised Land. We will even bring our children along. But, can we leave our material assets behind?

Pharaoh knows that, if their herds and flocks are left in Egypt, God's people will come back. Moses knows this too. We will sacrifice almost everything for material gain: our salvation, our sanctification, and even our children.

We will never be able to go to the Promised Land, if our material possessions don't also go with us. If our wallets and purses aren't owned by God, neither are our hearts. Nothing can be left behind in Egypt. Nothing is owned by Egypt. It all belongs to God or our faith lacks a seamless integrity.

DESERT REFLECTIONS

Job discovered that the seasons of suffering will test your integrity more than anything else. The devil reasoned that Job was righteous because he was rich. In short, Job served God because it paid to be good.

In an age of religious hucksters who sell a gospel that promises automatic blessings to those who serve God, you might be confused when bad things happen to good people. You might even think that God has abandoned you in the desert.

There is a goodness in your desert crossings. When tribulations come, they test your faith. Yet, when the pharaohs of this world tempt you to compromise in order to avoid the pain, you have a wonderful opportunity to discover whether you faith is real or not. When your faith triumphs in the face of temptation, you will be filled with the inexpressible joy of knowing that it is real and substantial.

You are being transformed even during the desert crossings as your integrity grows stronger and stronger.

DISAPPOINTMENT

DESERT 6

"We must accept finite disappointment, but never lose infinite hope."

Martin Luther King

Surely Andy understood disappointment. His ability to withstand pain became the stuff of frontier legend. Raised by a widowed mother in a hillbilly cabin, this freckle-faced runt learned early how to fight for everything he ever got. A nervous condition that caused him to slobber made him the target of cruel jokes. It also made him as tough as the hickory trees in his South Carolina forests.

At age 13, this tenacious teen ran off to fight in the Revolutionary War. Soon afterwards, he and his brother were captured. When he refused to shine the boots of a British officer, he was struck by a sword that left a vicious gash across his forehead. That blow would cause Andy a lifetime of migraine headaches.

During their imprisonment, the two brothers came down with smallpox. Their mother walked 45 miles to the British camp and somehow got her boys released. A few days later, his brother Robert died from the pox. Andy slipped into delirium and was unconscious when his mother died of cholera. He barely had time to digest his mother's death when news came that his brother Hugh had been killed in battle. Within weeks, he had lost his entire family. During those days of agonizing grief, he formulated a credo that would serve him well in the rough-and-tumble years ahead: "One man with courage makes a majority."

He rose from his bitter disappointments to attack life with a vengeance. When he wasn't fighting Indians, Andy was mixing it up in barroom brawls and deadly duels. It seemed that the hurt inside drove him to inflict pain on others.

Then he fell in love with Rachel. For the first time in his life, he was gloriously happy. But she was a divorcee, and he had big political dreams in an age when divorce was scandalous. After he married Rachel, they discovered that the courts had made a terrible mistake and she was still legally married to her first husband.

For years afterwards, his beloved Rachel would be the brunt of salacious gossip. Andy fought thirteen duels defending her honor. People joked that his body carried so many bullets that when he walked "he shook like a bag of marbles." A bullet lodged near his heart brought him a lifetime of excruciating pain, causing his body to shake uncontrollably from hacking coughs that left his handkerchiefs drenched with blood.

He overcame his physical and emotional pains to become America's greatest military hero in the War of 1812. He would often say to those closest to him, "Never take counsel with your fears." That credo was tested when he decided to run for President of the United States. The stakes were great in a country teetering on the edge of civil war. In one of the dirtiest political campaigns in U.S. history, Rachel's name was dragged through the mud as his opponents viciously portrayed her as a loose woman unfit to be the first lady of America. During that brutal campaign, Andy and Rachel endured further pain when their sixteen year-old adopted son died of tuberculosis.

But, with the toughness that had earned him the nickname Old Hickory, Andrew Jackson won that election in 1828. The joy of victory was short-lived. His Rachel, wounded by the smear campaign against her, suffered a fatal heart attack. A grieving Andy was sworn in at an inauguration that turned into a riot. His drunken frontier supporters trashed the White House. Newspapers across America gave Andy a new nickname: King Mob.

He overcame the bitter disappointment of those first days to serve two terms. Through dogged determination he managed to steer America away from civil war. He was the only president ever to wipe out the Federal Deficit. He then skillfully navigated the country through its worst depression.

He retired to Nashville to live out his pain-filled final years. His body was racked with hacking cough and his pillows stained with blood. During his last days, his migraine headaches were unending and his body bloated. At the end, he called his family and servants to his deathbed and spoke of the infinite hope that still endured from his greatest disappointment in life: "Heaven will be no heaven if I do not meet my wife there. I go to meet Rachel. Do not cry for me, dear children. Follow Jesus and I will see you all, both black and white, in heaven."

Disappointment humbles the haughty and softens the stubborn. Its pain is God's scalpel to remove that which keeps us from great character. There's not a single person that our Lord didn't use greatly without first hurting deeply. Andy Jackson would tell you life's disappointments are the stuff that make your resolve as hard as old hickory.

Moses' road to the Promised Land was paved with disappointments. He must have felt sucker-punched at a bitter lake called Marah. What do you do when you have danced in triumph on the banks of the Red Sea only to find yourself dying of thirst at Marah three days later? If you are Andrew Jackson, how do you respond when you win the presidency, only to lose the love of your life two weeks later? Those of us who are crossing the desert of disappointment can find hope and resolve in this principle:

FINITE DISAPPOINTMENTS PAVE THE ROAD TO INFINITE HOPE.

In the afterglow of the amazing miracle at the Red Sea, the Israelites are giddy with excitement. But after the celebration, reality sets in. Standing between them and their hope is the desert. But you can't get to the Promised Land without going through a string of deserts.

The odds against them are overwhelming. There are around 3.6 million Jewish refugees. Giving each family enough space, their camp would be about 10½ miles square. If the Israelites and their livestock were placed in a line 50 abreast, the length of that line would stretch back 100 miles, taking nearly 50 hours to pass the same point. It would require 160 railroad boxcars of food, and 1,080 tank cars of water just to meet their daily needs in the most desolate wilderness on planet earth.

God delights in putting us in impossible situations that force us to walk by faith, not by sight. But faith is easier right after a big miracle. So the Israelites blindly follow that old man whose raised staff has just parted the seas. Exodus 15:22 is a snapshot of their faith: "...and they went into the Desert of Shur. For three days they traveled in the desert without finding water." Though their tongues were swollen, they kept plodding forward with the faith they gained at the Red Sea.

Then a cry went up, "Water ahead!" and the stampede was on. Imagine the disappointment when the first to arrive began spitting water out in disgust. Bad news always spreads fastest. Within minutes everyone knew the water was undrinkable. Exodus 15:23 says that they gave that desert lake a new name: Marah. The Hebrew literally means "the place of bitterness." Every one of us has spent time at our own Marah. Some of us have camped there for years.

In Exodus 15:24 we read, "So the people grumbled against Moses..." Dancing had turned to disappointment. Unrealized expectation is always the root of disappointment. This wound doesn't heal easily. Visit Marah enough times and faith can become a mass of hardened scars. Marah turns people into cynics and skeptics. After Marah you are afraid to hope again. In a song from his Broadway musical Passion, Stephen Sondheim speaks for lots of folks: "Ah, but if you have no expectations you will expect nothing and accept everything and you will never be disappointed."

The Enemy of our Soul does his best work at Marah. If he can cause us to fear the pain of disappointment and abandon risky faith, we are doomed to fall by the wayside in the desert. To overcome Marah, we need to grasp these four transforming truths:

1. GOD POSITIONS HIS PEOPLE AT MARAH

One of Satan's lies is that God is with us in the good times, but has abandoned us in the bad. When Job was suffering, and his wife told him to curse God, he replied, "Shall we accept good from God, and not trouble?" (Job 2:8) He is saying that trouble comes from God. For people like Job, Moses, and Andrew Jackson, trouble is one of God's precious gifts. Even when we find ourselves at Marah because of our own sin or stupidity, God will bring good out of the bad.

Don't lose sight of those first key words in Exodus 15:22: "Then Moses led Israel..." God's people didn't just stumble onto Marah. They were led there by God's design. Three days earlier they were led to the Red Sea. When we talk about the dancing that took place after the Red Sea crossing, we need to remember the despair before the miracle took place. Moses had led them into a trap. Before them was the sea. Behind them was the Pharaoh's army cutting off all escape. Exodus 14:10 says of the Israelites, "They were terrified and cried out to the LORD..."

There is a recurring cycle in the Exodus that we see at the Red Sea: a problem creates panic, resulting in prayer, bringing in provision that leads to praise. Only three days later, it happens again at Marah. Notice that God's people don't immediately pray. Complaining always seems to be their first option.

That's why God has to put them through the same five-step cycle again and again: problem... panic... prayer... provision... praise. Remember, these Israelites are recent converts. It was only after they crossed the Red Sea that Exodus 14:31 says, "...the people feared the Lord and put their trust in him..." When they get to Marah, they are three-day-old baby believers and incoming freshmen in the Desert School of Faith. Moses has already earned his PhD degree in forty years on the desert. He's now beginning post-doctoral work in desert faith, but the rest of them are just novices.

God could have taken them to the Promised Land further north, on a weeklong journey along the Mediterranean Sea. But they were a slave rabble, untrained in the art of war. They needed to become a unified nation of warriors. Most of all, they needed to be infused with God's presence and power. That's why they had to stop at places like Marah and recycle their faith with problem... panic... prayer... provision... praise.

He puts us through the same cycle. It's too bad that we have to come to Marah before we are desperate enough to pray. We might wish that we didn't have to be bailed out of a hopeless situation before we are motivated to praise him, even to the point of dancing. But, until we grow up, we will go through the cycle. When we get to the point where we don't need problems and panic to drive us to prayer, and we don't need provision to motivate our praise, then we will truly enter our Promised Land. Until then, God will often position us at Marah.

2. THE LORD PROVIDES FOR HIS PEOPLE AT MARAH

Baby believers complain when life throws them a curve ball at Marah. Their leader could have gotten upset when, according to Exodus 15:24, "...the people grumbled against Moses..." Someone asked her pastor, "Do you ever feel like you are being eaten by sharks?" He replied, "No, but I feel like I've been gummed to death by minnows." Spiritual leaders wear themselves out trying to placate and please unhappy parishioners. Maybe that's why 18,000 discouraged clergy are dropping out of the pastorate in the U.S. every year.

We should stand in awe of Moses. How did he go the distance for over forty years with his unhappy congregation? The secret is in Exodus 15:25: "Then Moses cried out to the Lord..." Instead of placating parishioners, he went to the Lord. The best ministry any pastor can ever perform is to pray for his church. The best thing parents can do is to pray for their children. The most effective thing any politician can do is to pray for his country. God alone provides the answers at places like Marah. Look at the amazing answer that God gives Moses:

> "...and the Lord showed him a piece of wood. He threw
> it into the water, and it became sweet."
>
> *Exodus 15: 25*

On the surface it is the strangest of miracles. But look closer, and you find the heart of the gospel. Literally, the Hebrew language says that Moses threw a tree into the water. Maybe he ripped it down, or it was a dead tree lying there old and rugged on the ground. In that tree, I see the cross of Jesus.

Moses said to God, "My people are thirsty." And God replied, "Show them the Cross." It's the Cross that turns the bitterness of sin and failure into the sweetness of grace and hope. Before he died, Andrew Jackson wrote to friends that his hope in seeing Rachel again was bound up in the blood shed on the

Cross. He knew that it had purchased the heaven where his Savior and sweetheart waited.

The Cross is always the answer. That's why St. Paul said to his parishioners, "But we preach Christ crucified..." (2 Corinthians 1:23) He added, "For I resolved to know nothing while I was with you except Christ and him crucified." In Christ's cross work, the greatest need of our life was met: salvation from hell and eternal life with God.

Every smaller need is also provided at the Cross. Whenever you are at Marah, and life is filled with disappointment, look to the Cross and remember the words of St. Paul in Romans 8:32, "He who did not spare his own son, but gave him up for us all—how will he not also, along with him, graciously give us all things." Indeed, there is a tree to make sweet the waters of bitterness, and remind you that God will provide everything you need for the journey.

3. THE LORD PROTECTS HIS PEOPLE AT MARAH

After the tree sweetens the bitter water, God gives a wonderful promise:

> "There the LORD made a decree and a law for them, and there he tested them. He said, 'If you listen carefully to the voice of the LORD your God and do what is right in his eyes, if you pay attention to his commands and keep his decrees, I will not bring on you any of the diseases I brought on the Egyptians, for I am the Lord who heals you."
>
> *Exodus 15:25&26*

In verse twenty-five, we see that God "tested" his people

at Marah. How did he test them? Could it be that, in those bitter waters, he was replaying the first plague that took place in Egypt? When Pharaoh hardened his heart against God's command, the Nile River turned to blood. All life in the Nile died. Its water was undrinkable. Because the Nile was the source of all life in that desert nation, God was pronouncing a death sentence on Egypt.

It is a curse as old as the Garden of Eden: "In the day you eat of the [forbidden] fruit, you will surely die." (Genesis 2:17) Paul repeated it in Romans 6:23: "For the wages of sin is death." Some of us are at Marah because of our sins. Sin brings death and disease, even for believers.

But there is that tree that sweetens the bitter waters. Jesus hung on that tree. He took upon himself the curse: sin, poverty, disease, and death. He endured God's wrath in our place. We take our refuge beneath that tree as surely as those ancient Israelites hid under the blood of the sacrificial lamb smeared on their doorpost on Passover night.

God protects us in Christ. Maybe you are at Marah today because of sin and stupidity. Now you are drinking the bitter water of sin's consequences. Are you thirsting for righteousness? Look to the Cross. Run to the Resurrected Savior. Throw yourself into his arms. Put your future in his nail-scarred hands.

In Exodus 15:26, God promises, "For I am the God who heals you." I Peter 2:24 responds, "For by his stripes we are healed." Christ will not only heal you, he will protect you all the way to the Promised Land. He loves you too much to let you live like the Egyptians. If you don't pay attention to his commands and decrees, he will allow you to suffer the diseases of the Egyptians. But if you will die to your own desires and lusts, and follow him, you will not be making nearly as many frequent stops at Marah.

4. THE LORD HAS A PURPOSE BEYOND MARAH

There is life after disappointment. Exodus 15:27 says, "Then they came to Elim where there were twelve springs and seventy palm trees, and they camped there near the waters." God doesn't want us to drive down our tent pegs at Marah. Too many people camp at the place of their bitterness for years, fixated on past disappointments.

Have you ever watched a massive elephant chained to a stake that he can easily rip out of the ground? Trainers tether them to the stake when they are babies. The baby elephant grunts and pulls, trying to break loose. After several weeks, he gives up. Later he has grown into several tons of massive power, but is still shackled to a stake designed for a baby elephant. In short, he is a prisoner of past failures at shaking loose. Though he is now an adult, he still thinks like a baby. Some us are like those poor elephants, still shackled to the stake of past disappointments; still prisoners of how things used to be.

It's time to move on from Marah while we still have a chance. The best that life has to offer is still out there ahead of us. If we never leave Marah, we'll never get to Elim.

On the other hand, if we stay camped at an oasis like Elim, we will never get on to the Promised Land. There is an old Arab proverb: "Nothing but sunshine turns the world into a desert." Every moment of life cannot be joyful. The journey involves seasons of happiness and disappointments; crossing the desert and resting at the oasis; Marah and Elim. But the only place that ultimately matters is our Promised Land.

Jesus knows what we are facing. He's been to Marah. It wasn't easy to drink the bitter cup of his suffering. No one ever prayed harder than he did in Gethsemane. Yet he moved on to the agony of the Cross. And three days later, he moved on to the Resurrection. After that he moved on up in his Ascension. One day he will return as the King of kings and Lord of lords.

Andy Jackson, God may take your Rachel, but Jesus and she wait for you in heaven. And so take the faith risk, knowing that finite disappointments pave the road to infinite hope. Move forward remembering God's provision for today: at every Marah there is a Cross. Never forget God's promise for tomorrow: beyond every Marah there is an Elim.

DESERT REFLECTIONS

Only God and you know how many disappointments stab at your body and soul. But the next time you feel that pain, take out a $20 bill and look at the picture of Andrew Jackson. Remember his story, along with the lessons of Marah.

Maybe you could also find comfort in a line written by Dr. Martin Luther King. When he was incarcerated in the Birmingham jail, he smuggled out these words to his followers: "We must expect finite disappointment, but never lose infinite hope."

Andy Jackson would say "amen" to those words of Dr. King. He would tell you that hope, birthed out of disappointment, grows into the hard resolve of Old Hickory. Moses would nod his head and say, "I agree with those sentiments."

BOREDOM

DESERT 7

"No pleasure endures for long unseasoned by variety."
Valerius Publius

This gourmet food was first discovered in the Sinai Desert. It came with the morning dew. When the moisture evaporated under the rising sun, thin flakes like white frost appeared. These delicate honey wafers melted in the mouth. It was the world's most nutritious food, packed with everything needed for health and high energy.

When the Israelites first discovered it in the desert sands, they cried out in Exodus 16:15, "Manna?" which in Hebrew means "What is it?" God gave this ragtag rabble of ex-slaves a

glorious vision. But standing between Egypt and their Promised Land was the Sinai, the most desolate string of deserts on
planet earth. The odds were impossible that 3.6 million people
could survive a forty year journey that required the equivalent of
160 railroad boxcars of food and 1,080 tanker cars of water—
every day.

Manna was his provision for the vision, appearing supernaturally every morning for 40 years. At first they couldn't eat
enough whatisit. But when it became breakfast, lunch, and
dinner every day, 30 days a month, 360 days a year for forty
straight years, this delectable delight turned into daily drudg-
ery. Three servings of whatisit a day for forty years add up
to 43,200 straight manna meals.

If Mrs. Moses had a cookbook, there must have been a
section entitled 1001 Recipes for Manna. Instead of asking,
"What's for dinner?" they rolled their eyes and asked, "How
did you fix it? They boiled, baked, broiled, barbequed, breaded,
and buttered it. They ate it cold, hot, raw, sliced, diced, sautéed,
and puréed. They turned it into manicotti, mannaroni pizza,
McManna burgers, bamanna bread, bamanna pie, and bamanna
splits. You name it, they tried it. But it's impossible to create
enough variety in 43,200 manna meals. No dinner guests on the
Sinai ever said to their hostess, "More manna, please."

The old saying is cliché but true: "Variety is the spice of life."
The Renaissance poet Francesco Petrarch penned these acid
words, "Sameness is the mother of disgust..." Maybe that's why
predictability is the devil's playground.

In the very beginning, Adam and Eve became bored with a
steady diet of God's food. So the Serpent tempted them to spice
up their lives with forbidden fruit. A line in the novel The Fight
Club asks this provocative question: "Did perpetual happiness

in the Garden of Eden maybe get so boring that eating the apple was justifiable?" St. Paul reminds us that we are just as susceptible to boredom when it comes to God's food:

> "For the time will come when people will not put up with sound doctrine. Instead, to suit their own desires, they will gather around them a great number of teachers to say what their itching ears want to hear."
>
> *2 Timothy 4:3*

In an age of 700 cable channels, fast food stores on every corner, and a veritable smorgasbord of seductions, religions, entertainments, and moral options to spice up postmodern boredom, God has given us a steady diet for our Exodus. Like the ancient Jews, we might ask, "What is it?" Jesus answers,

> "I am the bread of life. Your forefathers ate the manna in the desert, yet they died. But here is the bread that comes down from heaven which a person may eat and not die. I am the living bread that came down from heaven. If anyone eats this bread, he will live forever. This bread is my flesh, which I will give for the life of the world."
>
> *John 6:48-51 NIV*

Eleanor Roosevelt said, "If life were predictable it would cease to be life." But Jesus is anything but predictable. Unlike manna, we can describe our Lord in the words of Lamentations 3:23: "For his mercies are new every morning." Jesus is the same yesterday, today, and forever. But his sameness brings spice with life.

When we are distracted by eye candy, and tempted to binge

on junk food philosophy with empty calorie morality, we have to grab hold of this principle:

CHRIST IS SUFFICIENT NOURISHMENT FOR THE WHOLE JOURNEY.

Adam and Eve lived in a lush forest of fruit trees providing an endless smorgasbord of good things to eat. There was only one forbidden fruit. God said, "In the day you eat it, you shall surely die." (Genesis 2:17)

When they put that forbidden fruit into their mouths, they reversed everything. Where there was once a paradise of good options with only one bad choice, there is now a wilderness of bad options with only one good choice—the Cross.

Where there was only one tree bearing bad fruit, there is now only one tree bearing good fruit—the Cross. Where only one tree brought death, now only one tree brings life—the Cross. The bread of heaven was nailed to it. The world says, "Whatisit?" But we know that the one who hung there is the food who alone gives and sustains our life.

When we first tasted his grace, it was amazing. We feasted on him like those ancient Israelites first gorged themselves on manna. But many of us have grown bored, going into nearby forests to feed on the forbidden fruits of strange doctrines, mindless entertainments, materialistic pursuits, and other substitutes for heaven's bread. Along with our ancestors in the Sinai, it is so easy to slip away from our Lord's Table.

Like Adam and Eve, our boredom turns our world into a desert. Perhaps you are crossing a desert of consequences that was created when your boredom with righteous living led you to eat forbidden fruit. Or you are tempted to pluck new fruit that will put you on a desert. If so, you need to grab hold of these three truths:

1. STARVING PEOPLE NEED FOOD FROM HEAVEN

Again, the road to our Promised Land always passes through a string of deserts because transformation is forged through tribulation. How does the desert do its work?

Remember Marah. The Jews were insatiably thirsty after their desert trek from the Red Sea to Marah. When they got there, they found undrinkable water. In the desert God makes them agonizingly thirsty. Now, after several weeks at the oasis of Elim, they are crossing another desert. The issue is no longer water. Now they face a second crisis. Listen to their loud wailing in the desert wind:

> "If only we had died by the LORD'S hand in Egypt. There we sat around pots of meat and had all the food we wanted. But you have brought us out into this desert to starve this entire assembly to death."
>
> *Exodus 16:3*

IN THE DESERT GOD ALSO MAKES HIS PEOPLE RAVENOUSLY HUNGRY.

When God puts us in the desert, we wish we could go back to Egypt. We remember the food while forgetting the bondage. Those Jews recall the Nile River that turned the North African desert into a garden. No one had to depend on God for food or drink. Because the Nile was their sustainer, they worshipped creation rather than the Creator.

When people are satisfied by the stuff of creation they forget their Creator. That's why Jesus said in Matthew 19:24, "It is easier for a camel to go through the eye of a needle than for a rich man to enter the kingdom of heaven." Do you see why God's first plague was turning the Nile into blood, making it undrinkable? He was declaring,

> "I AM the Creator. I AM alone the giver and taker of life. Your future is not determined by creation or the stuff it gives you. I AM alone creation's Master. I will turn off the faucet, and you will die of thirst and hunger."

God loves us best by removing the stuff we depend on most. Plagues come and we are stripped of money, family, friends, and health. The Nile turns to blood. The Red Sea is impassable. The waters at Marah are bitter. The desert after Elim offers no food.

It is during those times that God reminds us that nothing in creation can save us. The same Nile that quenched our thirst also birthed a civilization, enslaved and worked us to death. The same Nile that gave us pots full of meat was also the river where our babies were drowned. It suddenly dawns on us that things we get from creation exact a horrific cost for our children and us. Though the Nile may temporarily feed our bodies, it leaves our souls agonizingly thirsty and ravenously hungry.

THE SALVATION IN STARVATION

Thank God for deserts that wake us up to reality. In the 6th chapter of St. John's gospel, Jesus leads the crowds out into a barren wilderness. It is late afternoon and they are famished. All they have is a little boy's few fishes and loaves. There, Jesus miraculously turns that little lunch into a meal for as many as 20,000 people.

Jesus is setting them up for something bigger than a miracle. It is close to Passover and their mind is on the Exodus. So Jesus reminds them about the miracle of manna in the desert. He tells them that the manna didn't keep their ancestors from ultimately dying (nor will this meal of fishes and loaves). But he says in John 6:51, "I am the bread that came down from heaven. If anyone eats of this bread he will live forever."

Then, in John 6:53, he drops the bombshell: "I tell you the truth, unless you eat the flesh of the Son of Man, and drink his blood, you will have no life in you." It's at this point that Jesus loses most of his disciples. Maybe they think that he is telling them literally to eat his body. But he responds in John 6:63, "The Spirit gives life and the flesh counts for nothing." He is saying that we must spiritually feed on him. Even that is too much. Only his original twelve disciples manage to follow him after that.

It is at the point of feeding on Jesus that true disciples are separated from nominal believers. Remember the desert reduces us to thirst and hunger. To the thirsty he says, "Drink my blood." To the hungry he says, "Eat my flesh."

Nominal believers say, "I might follow you for some fishes and loaves to feed my body, and some water turned into wine to quench my thirst, and for miracles that fix my body. As long as you give me the things of creation, I'll be there with you." But Jesus is calling disciples to something more radical. He tells us to die to the things of creation, and eat the things of heaven. He is calling us to feed on the Creator. Only those who hunger and thirst for righteousness ever long for true soul food.

2. BEWARE OF PICKING AT YOUR FOOD

Exodus 16:35 reminds us, "The Israelites ate manna forty years, until they came to a land that was settled; they ate manna until they reached the border of Canaan." Again, that's 42,300 straight manna meals. Fast forward several years to Numbers 11:4: "The rabble with them began to crave other food, and again the Israelites started wailing." Again they wanted to go back to Egypt. Look at what they say next:

> "We remember the fish we ate in Egypt at no cost—also the cucumbers, melons, leeks, onions, and fish."
>
> *Numbers 11:5*

You have to be desperate to want a blue plate special like that! Notice two things: the deception. They said that the food of Egypt costs nothing. The truth is, it took everything—their freedom, dignity, wasted lives, and children.

The attraction. God gives one food—manna. The place of bondage offers a tempting variety. Notice there are six items mentioned in this Egyptian smorgasbord. In Hebrew numerology, six is the number of man. Egypt is just another installment of Babylon; another world system that offers to feed you, if only you will become its slave. Its number is 666. But God's number is 1. He offers one item to feed your soul and quench your thirst: His Only Begotten Son.

The Israelites cried out in Numbers 11:6, "But now we have lost our appetite; we never see anything but this manna!" Some of us have lost our appetite for Jesus. We are continually attracted to Egyptian food because we have swallowed the deception that it costs nothing. The truth is, it will cost us everything in this world, and eternity to boot.

God heard those complainers in the eleventh chapter of Numbers. Sometimes the worst thing God can ever do is to answer our prayers. In response to their wailing, he sent a wind that blew a massive migration of quail off course and into the desert. They fell by the millions and were clubbed to death by Israelites starved for meat.

But, even as they opened their mouths to devour the meat, they were eating death. The quail were carrying a deadly virus. Numbers 11:34 says, "There they buried the people who had craved other food." How many saints go to an early grave because of their lusts for the pleasures of Egypt? Worse than that, how many Christians wither up and die spiritually because they turn away from Jesus to pursue junk food theology, empty calorie pleasures, and eye candy rather than soul food?

Don't pick at the bread of heaven. Feast on it with gusto, remembering a verse from this old hymn: "Turn your eyes upon Jesus. Look full in his wonderful face. And the things of earth will grow strangely dim in the light of his glory and grace."

3. LEARN TO SPOT THE SIGNS OF SPIRITUAL BOREDOM

When they first discovered manna in the sixteenth chapter of Exodus, they were beside themselves with joy. Some thirty years and 32,400 manna meals later, Numbers 11:6 says that they had lost their appetite. A while ago, my wife Joyce and I went on a 30-day raw food diet. By the end of that month, we were ready to kill for a grilled piece of meat. After that, we could sympathize with those ancient Israelites. Raw food may be good for us, but it kills the appetite. Feeding on Jesus for years doesn't make the appetite for the world go away. Earthly things will tempt each of us until the day we are released from our sinful body. That's why we need to look at Exodus 16 to discover the three types of people who lose their appetite for heaven's bread:

THE OVERFED AND THE UNDERWORKED

God commanded his people to gather only enough for each day. They were to eat enough to exercise it off, and then go out and get a fresh batch of whatisit the next morning. Exodus 16:20 says that some of them grabbed a lot more than they needed.

There are a lot of Christians like that. They grab all of Jesus they can. They attend Bible studies, go to seminars, listen to CDs, watch DVDs, and stuff themselves. They become fat babies in the pew instead of lean warriors in the world.

The bread of heaven cannot be hoarded. Verse twenty says that the next morning the hoarded manna was "full of maggots and began to smell." There is a stench in the church when we stuff ourselves with Christ but never share the Living Word with the world. After a while we get fat and lethargic and boredom sets in.

THE OVERWORKED AND UNDERFED

This is the other extreme. Exodus 16:4&5 present the starved. They have trekked across the desert without food and are in desperate need of manna yet to be discovered. Some of God's people are trekking energetically through life, involved in all kinds of activities that benefit others. But though these activists do the work of Jesus, they don't feed on him. Working in their own strength, they wear out and burn out. Later, in Exodus 16:17 we read that some gathered only a little manna. There are believers who spend a little time feeding on Jesus in prayer, or a few minutes digesting his Word.

We see in Exodus 16:21-23 that they were allowed to gather a double portion the day before the Sabbath so that they wouldn't have to work on the Lord's Day. Some people come only on the Sabbath Day to get all their "Jesus feeding" for the week. They want a double portion on Sunday to live on for the other six days of the week. They live vicariously off others who are feeding on Jesus. They stand quietly and watch passively while the congregation shouts to the Lord. They feed off the passion of the pastor's sermon, but seldom feed themselves from the same Bible. No one is ever fed watching others eat. They become spiritually emaciated and fall in weariness by the wayside.

MALNOURISHED BUT DISCONTENT

We see the third group of God's people in the 11th Chapter of Numbers. Bored with Jesus, they crave the meat they had in Egypt. So God gives them what they want. Millions of quail fall out of the sky. They are buried in piles of meat.

This bored generation of Americans is like those ancient Israelites. We invent new ways to entertain ourselves to death in a media saturated age. We are up to our necks in quail. We feast on it 24/7. But it's full of empty calories. Worse than that, it carries deadly disease that has brought a plague on our culture and infected our churches.

What caused them to become enamored with the flesh pots of Egypt that they had left behind? Notice carefully the key phrase in the 11th chapter of Numbers. Verse one: "Now the people complained..." Again and again you read those words that describe their attitude: complain, grumble, criticize, wail, and whine. Look again at their complaint in verse six: "But now we have lost our appetite; we never see anything but this manna." Beware of a critical spirit: finding fault with your life, family, job, and church. Watch out when you begin to obsess on the negatives in your life. Beware of the spirit of always trying to fix others or yourself. A lack of gratitude and contentment with what God has given you will lead to the flesh pots of Egypt and a plague.

There's no greater stench in the nostrils of God than bored Christians. Jesus says in Revelation 3:16 that he will vomit the "lukewarm" out of his mouth. It's his way of saying that the bored believer makes him sick to his stomach. Beware of boredom. It is a desert that has no end.

DESERT REFLECTIONS

Dear saint, have you lost the first love that you had when you first discovered Jesus in the desert of your life? Back then, you hungered and thirsted after righteousness. When you first tasted Jesus, you couldn't get enough. But somewhere along the line, boredom set in and the fleshpots of Egypt beckoned.

May I challenge you to come back to the Table of Jesus with a thankful attitude? The ancients called it the Eucharist from the Greek word for thanksgiving. Thankfulness is not so much a feeling as it is an intentional discipline. Start by declaring a fast from quail. Turn off your television, put away your cell phones and cut back on some activities. Get back to the simple lifestyle that gives you enough time and energy to feed on Jesus. The Nike Slogan is perfect for times like this: **"Just do it!"**

RESENTMENT

DESERT 8

"Nothing on earth consumes a person more quickly than the passion of resentment."

Friedrich Nietzsche

No one would have guessed that Leonard Holt was a ticking time bomb. He had worked as a lab technician at the same Pennsylvania paper mill for nineteen years. He was respected as a Boy Scout leader, devoted father, member of the fire brigade, and regular churchgoer.

But on a cold October morning, Leonard stuffed a 45 automatic and a Smith and Wesson .38 in his coat pockets.

After driving to the mill, he stalked the shop while executing people he had known for more than fifteen years.

His community was left bewildered that a mild mannered man could become a mass murderer. An investigation pieced together a profile of seething resentment. Several of his victims had been promoted over him while he remained mired in the same position. Some of his car pool had quit riding with him because of his reckless driving. Holt had punched a neighbor after they argued over a fallen tree.

Resentment had been building up for years until it exploded in rage. Three words appeared beneath his picture in Time magazine:

RESPONSIBLE, RESPECTFUL AND RESENTFUL

Leonard Holt was a forerunner in what has become an all-too-common phenomenon of rage turning dorms, malls, playgrounds, and even churches into killing fields. We have invented a whole new lexicon of words to describe it: going ballistic; coming unhinged; doing a Columbine; going postal.

We may look with horror at suicide bombers in the Middle East. Yet every day in America, ticking time bombs walk among us. They don't always explode into a killing spree. But the marks of their rage are found in battered children, broken marriages, and souls withered by ugly, caustic words.

Resentment is anger stuffed inside. Christians are especially susceptible to this. We pretend that everything is okay, masking our hurt with God talk. But, pretending never heals pain. We may think that these smoldering embers of resentment are under control, but it only takes a sudden breeze to fan them into a wildfire.

A woman confessed to evangelist Billy Sunday, "I have a terrible temper, but it only lasts a few seconds." He replied, "Madam, a shotgun blast lasts but a moment, but it leaves behind a lifetime of ruin."

Even prophets like Moses can go postal. For more than thirty years he was a paragon of respectability. When everyone around him was coming unhinged, he stayed calm while enduring the insufferable grousing of 3.6 million crybabies. He couldn't remember how many times they threatened to stone him to death. Even his own family conspired against him. Yet he handled it all with uncommon grace and unflinching resolve. It was no exaggeration for Numbers 12:3 to record, "Now Moses was a very humble man, more humble than anyone on the face of the earth." But the line under Leonard Holt's picture in Time magazine could have been inscribed under a photo of Moses:

RESPONSIBLE, RESPECTFUL AND RESENTFUL

For years Moses stuffed his anger inside. When they came to yet another desert, the rabble began to complain again. The old man despised the whining of these sniveling ingrates. You would think that, after thirty years of never-ending miracles, they'd quit their whining. God patiently whispered to Moses in Numbers 20:8, "Speak to that rock before their eyes and it will pour out its water" Instead Moses went ballistic.

> "Moses said to them, 'Listen you rebels, must we bring you water out of this rock?' Then Moses raised his arm and struck the rock twice with his staff."
>
> *Numbers 20:10*

On the surface, it was another miracle. In fact, it was an ugly display of resentment. Moses may have hit the rock, but he was mentally whacking his parishioners. He might as well have been Leonard Holt shooting people in the shop. How seriously does God take Moses' outburst? He says to Moses,

> "Because you did not trust me enough to honor me as holy in the sight of the Israelites, you will not bring this community into the land I give them."

Numbers 20:12

Doesn't this seem monstrously unfair? For seventy years Moses has been faithful to God. By faith he walked away from a palace. By faith he endured forty years of lonely exile. By faith he stood up to the Pharaoh and freed 3.6 million slaves. For thirty years his faith led them across a string of deserts. And now, he forfeits his dream while those ingrates get to waltz into the Promised Land?

God's harsh judgment on Moses has puzzled saints down through the ages. There must be something far deeper than an outburst of rage. The truth is: what Moses did really is a big deal. In fact, it cuts the very heart out of the gospel. How we handle resentment says everything about whether or not we have grasped the meaning of our salvation in Christ. There are few things more critical for our faith journey than this principle for desert crossings:

....

NOTHING ON EARTH CONSUMES THE PROMISE OF LIFE MORE QUICKLY THAN THE PASSION OF RESENTMENT.

....

No one ever dreamed that Leonard Holt had a problem with resentment. And nobody dreams that we do either. At least not yet!

Hebrews 12:15 says, "See to it that no one misses the grace of God and that no bitter root grows up to cause trouble and defile many." The writer warns us that bitterness causes us to miss the grace of God. Grace and resentment cannot occupy the same space. That's why Ephesians 4:26&27 says, "Do not let the sun go down while you are still angry. And do not give the devil a foothold." Our ancient Enemy only needs an inch of resentment to establish a beachhead in our lives. What starts out as a root of bitterness will grow into a tangle that strangles grace and suffocates hearts. If we are going to prune those roots of resentment, we have to act on four transforming truths:

1. THE ROAD OUT OF THE DESERT GOES THROUGH THE DESERT

We have repeated this principle more than any other: the road to our Promised Land leads through the desert. God could have taken his people on the easy, short route along the Mediterranean Sea. But he needed to organize a mob into a nation, and grow moral pygmies into spiritual giants.

But, though the Israelites needed the desert, they didn't have to stay there forty years. They had a chance to go into the Promised Land earlier, but they didn't have the faith to possess it. So they had to wander through even more deserts. If we don't learn from past desert experiences, God has more waiting for us. His perfecting grace will not let go until it has accomplished its purpose to conform us to the image of Christ.

In today's episode of Exodus we see two desert experiences separated by 30 years. The first is in Exodus 17. The Israelites had only been following the Lord for three months. We are not surprised that they grumbled and cried out in verse three, "Why did you bring us up out of Egypt to make us and our children die of thirst?" But you would expect better of them thirty years later in Numbers 20. Instead, we read in verse 4&5, "Why did you bring the Lord's community into this desert, that we and our livestock should die here? Why did you bring us up out of Egypt to this terrible place?"

In the years since their first desert, they had seen at least 10,900 miracles. But their complaint is almost verbatim to what it was 30 years earlier. Their deserts have taught them nothing.

What is it that God wants to teach both Moses and his people? It is the same thing he wants to teach us all: amazing grace. Consider this question: If grace is at the heart of our faith, then what is the most mature way we can show it? Scripture would answer with one word: gratitude. The word gratitude comes from the Latin word gratia or grace. Grace is getting what we don't deserve. Gratitude is being thankful for it.

These Israeli slaves got what they didn't deserve: freedom and a Promised Land. They were fed every day in the desert. They were given one of the greatest leaders the world has ever seen. But they constantly criticized Moses. The truth is: they were criticizing the Lord who gave them their leader. When they complained about the desert, they were complaining about the God who led them there. Instead of saying grace over their daily manna, they groused about how boring it was.

And Moses had the same problem. God had showered him with grace too. He rescued him from exile and gave him the opportunity to lead history's greatest faith adventure. Moses performed spectacular miracles, talked to God face-to-face, watched the Ten Commandments being etched in stone, designed the tabernacle, wrote the first five books of the Bible, and shepherded God's people.

But he too was ungrateful. The people rejected him, and he resented them. They may have made their complaints to one another in public, but he repeatedly complained about them to God in private.

In Numbers 20:10 he screams, "Listen you rebels!" He might as well be yelling, "I hate you all!" He is cursing the very people that God has given to him as a gift. He doesn't even realize that he is repudiating the grace of God. So are we when we lash out at loved ones or complain about circumstances.

Are you a complainer—ungrateful for your spouse, your parents, your children, your circumstances, your church, or the way God has wired you? You might as well scream at heaven, "God, you made a mistake!" The desert is full of sourpuss Christians.

Do you want to get out of the desert? In the words of an old gospel hymn, you need to "...count your blessings, name them one by one; count your blessings, see what God has done..." Hebrews 12:2 says that "Jesus, for the joy set before him, endured the Cross..." In the end, we will only be transformed into the image of Christ when we have come to the place where we are grateful even to carry a cross through a desert for the glory of God.

2. BRING YOUR RESENTMENTS TO THE ROCK

In Exodus 17:3, the people lash out in resentment against Moses, "Why did you bring us up out of Egypt?" In Exodus 17:4, Moses lashes back in resentment against them, "What am I to do with these people?" Yet there is a big difference. They carry their complaints to one another. Moses carries his complaints to God. Are you harboring some resentment? Go to the Lord, and wrestle with him until the bitterness is gone.

Moses cries out, "How am I going to find water for these people?" God answers in Exodus 17:5, "Go to the rock." In verse six he says, "Strike the rock and water will come out of it for my people." So Moses struck the rock, and water came gushing out. This was pure grace on God's part. Neither Moses nor his people deserved it. Notice in Exodus 17:7 that Moses called that place Massah, which in Hebrew literally means, "The place of testing." There, the ungrateful people of God tested his patience.

But the gospel is also at this place called Massah. Look carefully and you will see the Cross. Throughout the Bible, God is referred to as "the rock of our salvation." Jesus is again and again referred to as the Rock. The hymn writer calls him the Rock of Ages.

Jesus came to earth because we have tested God with our sins. We had turned Eden into a desert of Massah. We hungered and thirsted for righteousness, but there was none to be found. So the Rock came to a hill called Golgotha. There he was hung on a tree. Our sins were placed on him. A Holy God exacted justice. He beat Jesus as surely as Moses struck that rock at Massah. The prophet Isaiah said, "He was wounded for our transgressions." One of his executioners jammed a spear into his side, and blood and water came gushing out. Jesus knew that was going to happen when he poured wine into the cup at the Passover Feast the night before his crucifixion. He said, "This cup is the new covenant in my blood which is shed for you."

At the rock of Massah, God gives a preview of the crucifixion. This is God's unmerited favor. Resentful and ungrateful people are given water that gushes from Christ's wounded side. They are forgiven because he has been struck and stricken in their place. Do you have any resentments? Bring them to the Rock. Lay them on Jesus. He alone bears the guilt, endures the punishment, and washes everything new.

3. DON'T HIT THE ROCK TWICE

Fast forward thirty years to a rock in another desert. The people are again testing God. They still haven't grasped the grace of God. Worse than that, Moses has lost sight of it. The spirit of Leonard Holt is stalking the camp. Some 30 years before, God told Moses to strike the rock. But now, in Numbers 20:8, he says, "Speak to the rock..."

Remember, Moses' staff is a symbol of God's power and judgment. This staff turns into a snake that devours. It spawns plagues and brings the seas crashing down on Pharaoh's army. When he struck the rock in the desert thirty years earlier, it was a picture of God's judgment on sin scourging Jesus on the Cross. But that only happened once in history. When Jesus cried, "It is finished!" God's wrath against his people was spent. Jesus was punished for every sin you ever commit, as well as every offense that any other believer commits against you.

At the heart of the gospel is an unalterable truth: the Rock never needs to be struck again! We don't have to beat ourselves up anymore, or beat up on those who have hurt us. We no longer have to nurse grudges against them as a silent form of getting even, or shut them out of our lives. To do so denies the Cross. "Vengeance is mine!" says the Lord, and he has beaten his Only Begotten Son with the rod of his vengeance.

So now Moses only has to speak to the rock. It's all any of us has to do when we come to Jesus. A simple prayer will bring all the grace won by his crucifixion for every need of our life. But when Moses hits the rock twice, he cut the very heart out of the gospel of grace. There is no greater sin that any Christian leader can commit than to remove grace from the gospel. Here's how Moses did it:

DISOBEDIENCE DENIES LOVE

God commanded one way, but Moses did it another. Jesus said, "If you love me, keep my commandments." (John 14:12) He repeated, "If you keep my commandments, you will abide in my love." (John 15:10) At the heart of grace is submission. There would be no grace if Jesus had not submitted to his Father's will.

When Moses pulled his staff back in disobedience to hit the rock, grace had already fled. It was gone the moment he cursed his people with, "You rebels!" Grace and disobedience are diametrically opposed. When a pastor doesn't submit to God's holy commands, when mom and dad don't submit to one another in love, and when God's people don't live in obedience to Christ, grace is hidden from those watching. Moses did a terrible thing to God's people that day!

A DOUBLE HIT DENIES GOD'S GRACE

Again, Christ died once and for all on that cross. When he cried, "It is finished!" it was finished. It was a day of unspeakable violence for Christ. Isaiah 53 uses pungent words to describe the brutality of his crucifixion: "sorrows; stricken; smitten; afflicted; pierced; crushed; wounded; oppressed; cut off." His punishment was enough for us, and everyone else. When Moses lashes out at the people, "You rebels!" and we lash out with piercing, caustic words at those who have hurt us, aren't we hitting Jesus again? Didn't Jesus already take enough verbal abuse at the cross?

When we get bitter at others or ourselves, and spend time mentally beating them or ourselves up, aren't we trying to crucify Jesus all over again? A second hit is redundant. It cuts the heart out of grace. Moses didn't need to hit the rock again to get water. He was hitting the rock because he wanted to hit those who had deeply hurt him. When we punish others, we have denied the work of the Cross and thrown the gospel overboard. Moses did a terrible thing that day, and so do we when our resentments drive us to get even.

WOE TO THE LEADER WHO BRINGS CONFUSION TO GRACE

As bad as striking the rock was, it was made even worse when he said in Numbers 20:10, "Listen you rebels, must we bring water out of this rock?" Focus on that pronoun we. It is a devastating statement. By saying we, he is claiming partial credit for what only God's miraculous power could do. Moses should never had said, "God and I did this together."

Woe to spiritual leaders who lift themselves up in the place of Christ, who promote their own talents and achievements, or act like they are indispensible to God's work. Sometimes, like Moses, we get resentful at slackers. We feel like we are carrying the whole load in the church, on the job, or in our marriage. Like Moses, we angrily cry out, "Do I have to do it all myself?" The moment those thoughts come to mind, we forget that Jesus is the rock of our salvation and his grace accomplishes everything.

There is no grace unless we can say, "To God alone be the glory!" Moses did a terrible thing when he stole a bit of God's glory and confused his followers about the meaning of grace.

RESENTMENT IS ALWAYS AIMED AT THE ROCK

When Moses struck the rock, he was really hitting God. The truth is: he was angry toward God for putting him in one bad situation after another. He was bitter at God for making him a nursemaid for a bunch of rebels. He was wishing that he never got the assignment of taking these ingrates to the Promised Land. Countless weary pastors, discouraged missionaries, undervalued church workers and underappreciated parents can understand Moses' resentment.

So God said, "Okay, I'll grant your wish. You aren't going in to the Land with those people you despise." Beware of ingratitude. If we complain long enough, God might just remove the glory from the church we groused about, or take away the pastor who could never satisfy us, or the spouse who never did enough, or the job that never paid enough, or even a Promised Land that has become a burden. Do you see what a terrible thing Moses did when he raised his stick against a gracious God?

IF YOU STUMBLE AT THE ROCK,
YOU CAN STILL STAND ON THE MOUNT

Hebrews 10:31 says, "It is a dreadful thing to fall into the hands of a Living God." God says to Moses in Numbers 20:10, "Because you did not trust in me enough to honor me as holy in the sight of the Israelites, you will not bring the community into the land I give them." God is holy. He will not allow us to drag his grace through the filth of our disobedience and ingratitude. There is nothing sadder than Moses going up alone to Mount

Nebo to die. It breaks our hearts to see him standing alone, watching his people going into Canaan without him.

If we leave the story there, we have forgotten the meaning of grace at the Rock. Grace was also sufficient for Moses. Fourteen hundred years later, Moses did enter the Promised Land. Matthew 18 tells us that he stood on a mountain in Israel with Jesus. This was the Lord who had first spoken to him out of the burning bush. The Great I AM had come in the flesh to redeem all the rebellious children of God. Now he was transfigured in glory, and a glorified Moses and Elijah stood there with him. Standing there in glory with Jesus had to be better than entering into the land with Joshua. Standing with Elijah was infinitely superior to standing on the other side of the Jordan with the rebels who had provoked him at the rock.

To see Moses standing in the Promised Land with our Savior reminds us of a great truth: no sin is so great that we can't take it to the rock of our salvation or keep us from finding the grace to continue on to our Promised Land!

DESERT REFLECTIONS

Leonard Holt reminds us that seething resentment can lurk in the shadows of respectability. Moses teaches us that even God's prophets are susceptible to meltdowns if resentments are allowed to fester. The incident at the desert rock teaches us that we can never predict when our internal seething will explode into an outburst. If we bear the name of Christ, we will give a mixed and confusing message about the gospel to the watching world. Though we may get some instant gratification from expressing our anger, the consequences can last a lifetime and beyond.

If your resentments continue to fester, you will turn your world into a desert crossing. When that happens, allow God to transform you from resentful to grateful—even if it takes another desert to make it happen. Remember, there is a Promised Land on the other side.

Because even faithful prophets get resentful, you will too. When it happens, deal with your resentments quickly before they suffocate your spiritual vitality and ruin relationships that matter most. Keep a short list of accounts. Settle matters according to the guidelines of Matthew 18. Discipline yourself to focus on the good things that God has given you by his grace, rather than nursing and rehearsing your disappointments.

Above all, when you stumble at the rock, remember Moses. At the same rock of his failure, he found grace. In the end, he stood on the mountain with his Savior. And so will you, if you grab hold of the Rock.

BUSYNESS

DESERT 9

"This generation is in a frenzy to fix everything that's wrong. It's no wonder that a society with urgency as its emblem has Valium as its addiction."

David Zach

The coal miner's son could never please his father. His mother loved her little Marty with the uncomplicated affection of a simple country peasant. But his brutish father often berated and bullied him. No matter how hard he tried, the boy could never satisfy his demanding dad.

In his angst to earn his father's approval, this coal miner's son became a manic perfectionist. He also turned into a religious zealot. If he couldn't satisfy his earthly father, maybe he could please his heavenly Father. Tragically Marty's God became the mirror image of his angry dad.

To placate his coal miner father, he went off to college and then law school, where he drove himself to earn top honors. He was also scandalized by the rowdy behavior of his classmates. He constantly complained that his school was more like a whorehouse and beer parlor than a university.

To placate his heavenly Father, he made a promise that he would never succumb to such carnal pursuits. He took a vow of chastity. When he was tormented by youthful lusts, he rolled naked in thorn bushes and submerged himself in the frigid waters of an ice-covered pond near his dormitory.

While traveling through thick forests one day, he was caught in a violent storm. As lightening danced about him, he was sure that the God of vengeance was about to exact retribution for his sins. He screamed into the howling wind, "God, if you spare me, I promise to become a monk!" After the storm, he left law school and entered seminary. His furious father never forgave Marty.

Nevertheless, the coal miner's son threw himself into the monastic life with a perfectionist's frenzy, fastidiously keeping all the rules. He later wrote, "If anyone could ever get to heaven by being a good monk, surely it would be me."

He was determined to become a theologian who would make God proud. In record time, he earned his doctorate in theology. He was elected to the faculty of his nation's premier university where he became a prolific writer. He gave alms to the poor, and worked tirelessly to improve the living conditions of peasants. But none of that calmed the angst in his guilt-ridden psyche. Years later he confessed, "I lost touch with Jesus as

Savior and Comforter, and made him the jailor and hangman of my pour soul."

A frantic Marty went on a pilgrimage to Rome where he hoped to find his salvation. Instead of holiness, he found debauchery. Disillusioned, he found his way to some rough-hewn marble steps known as Pilate's Stairs. Like millions of other pilgrims, Marty crawled up and down that sacred stairway trying to absolve his sins. He kissed each stone and cried out, "Pater Noster—Our Father!" He couldn't remember how many times he climbed up and down those steps on lacerated elbows and knees before he finally collapsed.

Then the little boy, who could never please his coal miner father, died. The monk, who could never do enough to please his heavenly Father, was born again. As he lay exhausted, he famously cried out words that have echoed down the corridors of time:

"The righteous shall live by faith alone!"

When Martin Luther uttered those words, he ignited the spark of what would become the Reformation. Five hundred years later, we are desperately in need of the same kind of reformation.

Marty was a fixer. He tried to fix things with his coal miner father. He tried to fix his inadequacies before God. He tried to fix others. Moses was a fixer too. As we shall see in Exodus 18, he wore himself out trying to fix his world. Most us are also fixers. But God has called us to evangelize the world, not fix it. It's not our job to play Holy Spirit. In the movie Rudy, a priest says, "I've learned two things in life: there is a God, and I'm not him." Fixers everywhere ought to heed the warning that Jethro gave to his son-in-law, Moses in Exodus 18:18:

"The work is too heavy for you; you cannot handle it alone."

The desert crossings to your Promised Land will take enough out of us without our taking on the burden of trying to fix everyone else. This principle from Exodus 18 can liberate fixers everywhere:

....

NONE OF US HAS ENOUGH TO DO ENOUGH TO FIX ENOUGH. ONLY GRACE IS AMAZING ENOUGH TO FIX ALL THAT IS BROKEN.

....

Moses was a compulsive fixer saddled with 3.6 million people who desperately needed to be fixed. No leader has ever been faced with a more daunting task than Moses. He had about forty years to turn anarchists into citizens, social outcasts into strong families, and a mob into a nation. All of that had to be done while getting this mass of cantankerous humanity across the most desolate deserts on planet earth.

We can understand why Moses feels overwhelmed. It's only been three months since they left Egypt, and already the wheels are coming off. Exodus 18:13 says that people stood in endless lines everyday waiting for Moses to fix their broken lives. And it was taking its toll. Jethro warned Moses in Exodus 18:18, "You'll only wear yourself out."

Martin Luther exhausted himself trying to fix what he couldn't fix. Futurist David Zach writes about us, "This generation is in a frenzy to fix everything that's wrong." But none of us has enough to do enough to fix enough. Luther's life was transformed when he realized that only grace is amazing enough to fix all that is broken. Moses discovered the following truths, and so can we:

1. IN THE SHADOW OF SINAI, YOU CAN NEVER DO ENOUGH

People reduce Exodus 18 to Jethro teaching Moses effective organizational strategies. It is far deeper than that. This incident in Moses' life reveals the heart of the gospel: what it means to live by grace rather than works.

Look at the context of this story. The Israelites are camped on the edge of the Desert of Sinai. They can see Mount Sinai towering in the distance. Within days they will trek toward that mountain. Sinai will become the seminal experience in Jewish history. At Mt. Sinai Moses will receive an endless minutia of detailed instruction on feast days, dietary restrictions, animal sacrifices, and rules governing every aspect of life. At the heart of this list of laws is the Ten Commandments.

Jesus summed up the Law in two commands: "Love the Lord your God with all your heart and with all your soul and with all your strength and with all your mind; and love your neighbor as yourself." (Luke 10:27&28)

As much as Mt. Sinai towers over the Jewish encampment, so does the Law of God. What motivates Moses? Even though he hasn't yet received the Law in stone, it is already written on his heart, as it is on all our hearts: "love God with everything you have, and love your neighbors as yourself."

But, if we embrace the Law, it will break our hearts. We won't be able to stand it if we don't love God enough. It will crush us when we see folks not loving God enough. We will weep when we see others in trouble. We will want to fix broken lives. In fact we will wear ourselves out, and then go to bed at night discouraged that we didn't do enough to love God or others. That's what Moses and Martin Luther did. After exhausting her life helping the poor, Mother Teresa of Calcutta wrote that she was driven to suicidal despair because she hadn't done enough to love God or others.

The Law of God is a good thing. Imagine the paradise this world would be if we could manage to keep the Ten Commandments. Unhappiness would cease if people really loved God and their neighbors. But here's the problem: the Law is good, but we aren't. St. Paul says in Romans 7:25, "So then, I myself in my mind am a slave to God's law, but in the sinful nature a slave to the law of sin." There's too much sin in us to fulfill the demands of the Law. It will break your heart as surely as it shattered Moses, Martin Luther and Mother Teresa. None of us has enough to do enough to fix enough.

Moses discovered that he couldn't even fix himself. Jethro watched Moses exhaust himself trying to fix the problems of 3.6 million Jews. He asked Moses in Exodus 18:14, "Why do you alone sit as judge, while all these people stand around you from morning till evening?" Like Moses, we too sit as the judge of those around us. We know exactly what our spouse should do to make our marriage better. Put us in charge of the church, and things would get better. Put us in the Oval Office, and we would get this country humming again. Most of all, we are addicted to dispensing advice to others.

Moses answered Jethro in Exodus 18:15, "Because the people come to me to seek God's will." Like Moses, we think that we are indispensible to others. But look at Jethro's response to Moses in verse eighteen: "The work is too heavy for you; you cannot handle it alone." Moses needs to come to grips with his own limitations, and so do we. After spending a lifetime trying to fix himself, St. Paul admitted in Romans 7: 24, "What a wretched man I am! Who will rescue me from this body of death?"

If we can't fix ourselves, surely we can't fix others. Exodus 18:13 says, "The people stood around from morning to evening." The line leading to Moses' tent hardly moved. In verse 18, Jethro captured the impossibility of trying to meet everyone's needs: "You and those people who come to you will only wear yourselves out. The work is too heavy..."

Pastors can go weeks on end without taking a single day off, and still go to bed every night feeling guilty that they didn't do enough. Mother Teresa was tormented by suicidal guilt in spite of her herculean efforts to alleviate poverty in the slums of Calcutta. No one performed more miracles than Jesus. Yet, when he returned to heaven, he left behind plenty of unhealed people.

It's okay if we can't fix everyone. Does that mean we give up helping others? No! Like Jesus, we use our brief time on this earth to love God and as many others as we can. Luther wrote, "Even if I knew that tomorrow the world would go to pieces, I would still plant my apple tree."

If we can't fix others, we can't fix our own family. The first lines of Exodus 18 tells us that Moses' wife and boys went to visit his father-in-law who lived nearby. Soon Mrs. Moses came back along with her father. Jethro had come to rescue his son-in-law for the sake of his daughter and grandchildren.

Like a lot of spiritual leaders, Moses was spending so much time fixing everyone else's problems that he was neglecting his own family. Every pastor's family knows the pain that Moses' wife and kids were feeling. But even perfect parenting isn't a guarantee of success. The greatest faith heroes in the Bible had children who didn't walk with God. The best of spouses and parents don't have enough to fix the sins embedded in their families.

Above all else, we can't do enough to please God. In Exodus 18:17 Jethro says to Moses, "What you are doing is not good." God has called Moses to lead these people. And now God uses Jethro to tell him that he's not doing a good job. And that is the ultimate problem with God's Law. We might do enough to please some of the people some of the time. We might even be pleased with ourselves as we work ourselves into exhaustion. But we will always fall short of the glory of a perfect God.

2. ONLY GRACE WILL FIX WHAT IS BROKEN

We might all wish we could love God and others enough to fix all the problems in ourselves and in our world. All of us on the ragged edge need to listen to Jethro when he shows Moses a better way directly from heaven:

> "Listen now to me and I will give you some advice, and may God be with you. You must be the people's representative before God and bring their disputes to him."
>
> *Exodus 18:19*

You see the first distinction between Law and Grace: "May God be with you." The Law says, "You must be with God." Grace says, "God will be with you." The Law says, "You must come up to Mt. Sinai to find God." Grace says, "God comes down from the heights of heaven to find you."

Jethro is calling Moses to a ministry of prayer. That too is grace. The Law says, "You have to carry the load." Grace says, "God will carry the load." What is prayer? It is a recognition that we can't fix ourselves. We can't fix others. We can't fix our marriages. We can't fix our churches. We can't fix our culture. We can't fix our nation. We can't fix what is broken in our world.

So we bring our burdens to God and lay them at his feet. At Mt. Sinai, the Law of God dumps a load of backbreaking requirements on us. Like Moses, we are left worn out. For all our efforts, everyone is still unhappy with our inability to meet their expectations. At Mt. Calvary, Jesus shoulders the load of righteousness we can't fulfill, pays for sins we can't repay, and meets needs we can't meet. That's amazing grace.

The Law says, "Love God with all your heart, soul, strength and mind. Love your neighbor as yourself." Grace says, "God loves you with all his heart, soul, strength, and mind. God loves you as much as he loves himself."

When we pray to receive Christ as our Lord and Savior, we are saying, "God, I can't manage my salvation. So I bring my sins and lay them at your feet." Every prayer afterwards is a confession that only his grace is sufficient. Martin Luther said to his wife, "I've got so much to do today, so I will begin by spending three hours in prayer." He said to his students, "Pray and let God worry." The Law is going to bed at night worrying how to fix things. Grace is sleeping through the night while God does the fixing. Pastors serve their churches best by giving their first priority to prayer. Parents love their children most by giving their first energy to praying for them. Politicians serve their constituents most effectively by prayer, because only God can fix a broken world.

3. TRANSFORMED BY GOD,
WE BRING TRANSFORMATION TO OTHERS

Jethro goes on in Exodus 18:20, "Teach them the decrees and laws, and show them the way to live and the duties they are to perform." Having prayed, Moses' second priority is to teach. When he comes into God's presence, he will receive God's instructions. After that, he is to pass them on to the people.

Jethro establishes the greatest principles of spiritual leadership: we cannot pass on to others what we don't already possess. But it's not enough for spiritual leaders to teach people the Law of God. If they tell people how to love God and others, they have only informed them. Even if they get passionate about it, they have only inspired them. Teaching alone will not transform. St. Paul refers to it as "the foolishness of preaching."

The book of Exodus tells us that every time Moses went up Mt. Sinai to see the LORD, he came back with the radiance of God's glory all over his face. But it would soon fade. So Moses put a veil over his face to hide the fading glory. And so it is with us. We have spiritual mountaintop experiences. A sermon inspires us, a Bible study enlightens us, a worship service fills us with joy, or we go on a mission trip that takes us to a new level. But the glory soon begins to fades.

Pollster George Barna states that 75 percent of Evangelicals say that they haven't had a meaningful spiritual experience in the last year. So preachers try to jazz up their congregations, pleading with them to love God more. They exhort their parishioners to work harder, tithe more, serve more, and do more. They don't even realize that they are preaching the Law that condemns rather than grace that transforms. No wonder we see little or no revival or reformation.

But New Testament Christianity is called to a greater ministry than Moses. Ours is Grace, not Law. The only time Moses ever kept the glory was in Matthew 17, fourteen hundred years later when he stood with Jesus on the Mount of Transfiguration. Grace alone transforms. St. Paul writes in 2 Corinthians 3:17, "And we, who with unveiled faces all reflect the Lord's glory are being transformed into his likeness with ever increasing glory." When we focus on Jesus, we are looking at grace.

How is grace preaching different from what Moses taught from the dictates of Mount Sinai? It focuses on God's love, not ours. It is about his work, not ours. Rather than saying, "Love God more!" it says, "God loves you even more!" Rather than saying, "Try harder and give more!" it says, "Jesus did enough!" It gives all the glory for our salvation and sanctification to God alone.

And what happens when we focus on the love of God? John 4:19 tells us: "We love him because he first loved us." The more we focus on his grace, the more we are transformed into his likeness. Martin Luther wrote, "We are saved by faith alone, but faith that saves is never alone." Transformation comes when we apprehend his grace. It produces a never-fading holiness of love that draws others to his transforming grace.

4. GRACE COMMUNITIES
TRANSFORM GRACELESS CULTURES

Jethro ends with a third priority in Exodus 18:24: "But select capable people..." He goes on to put together an organizational plan where laity takes over the ministry." No mere mortal, even if empowered with Christ's presence, can carry the load alone. We all have to band together. Even when Jesus faced the horrors of Gethsemane, he needed his disciples to stay near and pray with him. When they abandoned him in his hour of need, the angels came to minister to him. If Jesus needed others, his people surely need to form grace communities where they can share strengths and weaknesses.

Law says we have to fix ourselves. Grace says that we can lean on each other. A grace-filled church is filled with people who can admit their weaknesses, and are grateful to be dependent on the graceful help of others. Grace-filled congregations understand that everyone has been gifted by grace to advance the kingdom of God. Together, we share the burdens and fix the problems through mutual dependence on grace. Grace even says we can allow each other to mess up because God will fix mistakes. He alone will see us across deserts to the Promised Land!

DESERT REFLECTIONS

There is a wonderful line in the movie Hope Floats: "Adulthood is spending the rest of your life getting over your childhood." Even after his conversion experience, Martin Luther wrestled with his propensity toward perfectionism. Dysfunctional patterns are hard to break. Perhaps you are a recovering fixer. Take heart, my friend. Don't let your perfectionism cause you to become discouraged with your perfectionism.

Relax, and enjoy the journey. Take one step at a time. Keep returning to the priorities of prayer and meditation on God's Word. Spend time in his presence and find a community of grace where burdens are carried together.

Above all, don't allow Satan to tempt you to try to live the Christian life in the strength of your flesh. Martin Luther warned, "Wherever the Lord builds a cathedral, the devil builds a chapel." Satan's favorite hunting ground is the church. One of his diabolical strategies is to get God's people caught up in the unending busyness of religious activity so that they no longer have the time or energy for fellowship with their Creator. Sometimes, even church activity can become creation worship. Inevitably grace flies out the window, and soul weariness slithers in to suffocate life.

LONELINESS

DESERT 10

"Loneliness was tough, the toughest role you ever played.
Hollywood created a superstar, and pain was the price
you paid..."

Elton John's *"Candle in the Wind"*

Police found her entangled in her bed sheets next to a telephone dangling by its cord. Before she died, she had frantically tried to make one last phone call.

Folks in her hometown always said that the Mortenson girl would end up dead before her time. They also knew that she wasn't really a Mortenson girl. Her mother Gladys had conned Martin Mortenson into marrying her to hide an unwed pregnancy. The Mortenson girl never knew who her real dad was. When she was a baby, her mother walked out on Martin, leaving her daughter to grow up fatherless.

The little girl was only six years old when Gladys was carted off to an insane asylum. She spent the next ten years being shuffled through foster homes. In one, a foster father sexually abused her. In another, an older boy raped her. In a third, a renter molested her. Afterwards he said, "Here, honey, take this nickel and don't tell anyone what I did." When she told her foster mother, the woman screamed, "What did you do to lead him on? You had better not tell anyone! He pays his rent and we can't afford to lose his money." She later said, "I found out at an early age that I was only worth a nickel."

Even after she grew up to be a Hollywood goddess, she saw herself as little more than an object of men's fantasies. She told a reporter, "All I want is to be loved for myself." Yet Norma Jean Mortenson was always reinventing herself. As a child she adopted her mother's maiden name and became Norma Jean Baker. She turned into Norma Jean Dougherty when she got married at age sixteen. Later she wed America's baseball star and became Norma Jean DiMaggio. After she married a world-renowned playwright, they drank a toast to Norma Jean Miller.

When she was a 21-year-old model, a Hollywood publicist gave Norma Jean her most famous name, Marilyn Monroe. In more than thirty films she parlayed her "ditzy sexy blond" persona into stardom. But she felt used and dirty, like a molested little girl. She cynically said, "In Hollywood, a girl's virtue is worth less than her hairdo." She added, "They pay you a thousand dollars for a kiss and fifty cents for your soul."

She plowed through three failed marriages, numerous

unhappy romances, and secret affairs with the President of the United States and the Attorney General. She sadly confessed to a friend, "I'm just a small girl in a big world trying desperately to find someone to love." Toward the end of her life, a disillusioned Norma Jean said, "A wise girl kisses but doesn't love, listens but doesn't believe, and leaves before she is left." Though millions idolized her, she confided to a friend, "It's all make believe, isn't it?"

At age 36, her life was spiraling out of control. On her last night alive, she called actor Peter Lawford. She talked incessantly about how unloved she felt. Finally Lawford said, "Marilyn, I have enough troubles of my own," and abruptly hung up on her. Popping lethal barbiturates, she frantically dialed her phone, trying to find someone who would listen. When police discovered her lifeless body the next morning, her phone was dangling by her bed.

Claire Boothe Luce, the former editor of Vogue and Vanity Fair magazines, wrote about Norma Jean's suicide. She asked, "What really killed this love goddess who never found love?" Luce believed that the answer was that dangling telephone: "Marilyn Monroe died because she never got through to someone who would love her." She concluded, "Millions of people are dying because they can't get through to someone who loves them."

Elton John's megahit, Candle in the Wind, memorialized Norma Jean with this line: "Loneliness was tough, the toughest role you ever played." Loneliness is the toughest role that any of us will ever play. An MTV poll discovered that forty-five percent of 15-24-year-olds feels lonely "most of the time." A 2008 George Barna poll found that two-thirds of Evangelicals feel lonely even while at church. Claire Boothe Luce was right:

millions of people are dying because they can't get through to someone who loves them.

Marilyn Monroe's dangling phone is so tragic. If only she had called God. He knows all the lonely people. Do you know how much he loves us? Come to Mt. Sinai and see for yourself. Thirty four hundred years ago God came down and etched a love letter in stone. In this love letter from our heavenly Father, we are told how to love God and one another.

But, even as Moses was getting that love letter, the people below were already groveling before a golden calf. God cries from the mountaintop, "I desperately love you, and want you to love me and your neighbors the same way." The people scream back, "We want to love ourselves and gods of our own making!"

Thirty four hundred years later we still don't know how to love God or others. That's why we destroy the Norma Jeans of the world. In an age of loneliness, how will we ever live out God's Law of Love? The answer is in this old children's rhyme:

The Law commands, but gives neither feet nor hands;
The Gospel calls us to fly and gives us wings.

When Moses saw the people worshipping the golden calf, he angrily threw the tablets to the ground, breaking them to smithereens. Those stone shards were a picture of God's broken heart. Think about all the hearts shattered because people refuse to love the way the Ten Commandments tell us to love. God's law is good, but we are bad. The Law can tell us how to love, but can't give us the power to do it. So the love letter becomes an unbearable burden—as hard, cold, and heavy as those stone tablets Moses lugged down the mountainside.

That's why we need the gospel of grace. John Bunyan, the writer of Pilgrim's Progress, wrote a verse to teach this truth to children:

Run, John run, the Law commands.
But gives neither feet nor hands.
Better news the gospel brings.
It bids me fly and gives me wings.

For the sake of all the lonely, broken people like Norma Jean, let's see if we can find the wings to soar on winds of grace. Maybe these five truths will help:

1. WHEN WE CAN'T CLIMB UP HIS MOUNTAIN, GOD CLIMBS UP OURS

In the nineteenth chapter of Exodus the Israelites are now encamped at Mt. Sinai. Soon Moses will climb to the summit to meet his LORD face-to-face. In Exodus 19:4&5, God says to the Israelites,

"You yourselves have seen what I did to Egypt, and how I carried you on eagle's wings and brought you to myself...you will be my treasured possessions..."

These are the words of a passionate lover. But Mt. Sinai is one scary place. In Exodus 19:12 Moses is told to put a fence around the mountain. Any person or animal that touches the mountain will die. When God visits, it is no trifling matter. We read in verse sixteen, "Everyone in the camp trembled." We glibly say that we want the presence of God to fall on us. But this is what happens when God shows up:

"Mount Sinai was covered with smoke because the Lord descended on it in fire. The smoke billowed up like smoke from a furnace, the whole mountain trembled violently, and the sound of the trumpets grew louder and louder."

Exodus 18:18&19

A New Testament writer adds in Hebrews 12:21, "The sight was so terrifying that Moses said, 'I am trembling with fear.'"

What message is God giving his people at Mt. Sinai? The key is a little phrase tucked away in Exodus 19:23: "...the people cannot come up..." Earlier Moses told the people to clean themselves thoroughly, but they couldn't get themselves clean enough to stand in the presence of his glory. He told them to abstain from sex, but they still couldn't get themselves holy enough. Any one who even touched the mountain had to die. This is the demoralizing fact: if we cannot even touch that which God has touched without profaning it, how can we even presume to touch God himself? No wonder Hebrews 10:31 says, "It is a dreadful thing to fall into the hands of the living God."

In Psalm 24:3, King David asks two questions: "Who may ascend to the hill of the LORD? Who may stand in his holy place?" His answer in Psalm 24:4 is devastating: "He who has clean hands and a pure heart, who does not lift up his soul to an idol, or swear by what is false." In short, no one can ascend to the hill of the LORD! There's not one of us whose hands are clean enough, hearts pure enough, or conduct righteous enough to come up into his presence.

Mount Sinai thunders a warning: if you touch this consuming fire of a God, you will be instantly incinerated by his glory. This is no Huggy Bear God. Moses knows that if he survives this LORD, it will be by grace alone. Grace finds a way to do what the Law can't accomplish. When we couldn't ascend the holy hill to God, he came down to us. When we couldn't take on his glory, God took on our flesh. When the unclean couldn't touch his holiness, the holy one touched our uncleanness.

Thank God for a mountain outside Jerusalem. It's fitting that it looks like a skull, for it is a place of death. Appropriately, this rock formation sits in a garbage dump. There the refuse of humanity is crucified by the Romans at this place called Mt. Calvary. Though we are unable to climb Mt. Sinai bearing his glory, he was willing to climb Mt. Calvary bearing our sin. If we touched Mt. Sinai, our sin would profane his holiness and we would die. When he touched Mt. Calvary, his holiness sanctified our sin and he died.

It was the great exchange: he bore our sin so that we could be clothed in his righteousness; he endured the wrath of God so that we could enjoy the grace of God; he died so that we might live; he descended into hell so that we might ascend into heaven.

At Mt. Sinai, God commanded us to love, but he didn't give us the arms or legs to ascend to his glory. At Mt. Calvary he showed us how to love, and paid the penalty for our refusal to love. But if we are ever going to be able to love God and our neighbors the way he loved us on Mt. Calvary, we must look to a third mountain. It's on the edge of the Valley of Armageddon in Israel. The locals call it Mt. Tabor.

The seventeenth chapter of Matthew tells us that, a few weeks before his crucifixion, Jesus took some of his disciples up on that mountain. For a dazzling moment, he was transfigured in all his glory, giving a sneak preview of what he would be when he ascended back to heaven after his death, burial, and resurrection. Those disciples saw something of the great glory of God that was on Mt. Sinai 1400 years earlier. And standing there on Mt. Tabor with Jesus was Moses in his resurrected glory. It is when we stand with Jesus, filled with his resurrected presence and power, that we will be transformed into his glory. Only the gospel calls us to fly and gives us wings. Have you trusted in his finished work on Mt. Calvary? Have you asked him to fill you with his presence and power so that you can ascend to the holy hill of God?

2. BEFORE WE LOVED HIM, HE ALREADY LOVED US

Moses is about to receive the Commandments telling God's people how to love their Father in heaven and their neighbors on earth. But first God says in Exodus 20:2, "I am the LORD your God, who brought you out of Egypt, out of the land of slavery."

Before he tells them to love him, he reminds them that he has already loved them. He never says, "I'll love you if you first love me or only after you love me, or to the extent that you love me." He loved them when they were still in love with the gods of Egypt. He remembered them when they had forgotten him. He felt their pain when they complained that he didn't care. He set them free even as they criticized him for the way he did it. His love is unconditional.

Remember the night that the Death Angel passed over Egypt. God was punishing the Egyptians for their disobedience. St. Paul wrote in Romans 6:23, "For the wages of sin is death." The Jews hadn't been obedient either, but they obeyed the one command that mattered when they killed their lambs and smeared the blood on the doorposts of their houses. By putting themselves under the blood of the lamb, they were saved that night.

It is no accident that the firstborn sons of Egypt were killed. God is reminding us that the lambs were a picture of his Son. When you hear the weeping in Egypt, you hear the weeping of a loveless and lost world. You also hear the weeping of your Father in heaven, the day God's Only Begotten Son and Lamb suffered and died on Mt. Calvary so that his blood could wash away the sins of our Father's lost sons and daughters.

God begins by declaring his love before he asks for our love. In Exodus 20:2 he is saying that his grace takes precedence over his law. Mt. Calvary towers over Mt. Sinai. How will we ever manage to love God and our neighbors? 1 John 4:19 gives the secret: "We love him because he first loved us." Either we will focus on what we have to do, or on what he has already done. Either we will beat ourselves up because we haven't done enough, or we will rest in the fact that he has done it all. We will love him and others out of gratitude, not a sense of obligation. Grace will give us the wings to soar.

3. LOVE'S DEFINITION IS ETCHED IN GOD'S LAW

Love is not a Hallmark Card feeling. It has substance and definition. We don't have to grope around in the dark trying to figure out how to love. In the first four commandments of Exodus 20:3-11, we are told how to love our God with all our heart, soul, strength, and mind. The order of the commandments is critical. We will never love our neighbors until we love ourselves, and we will never love ourselves until we are in a passionate relationship with the God who loves us.

So God begins by focusing on the way we are to love him. Verse three says, "You shall have no other gods before me." God is to take first place in our life. Nothing else is to come between him and us. Remember, that's how he loves us. Not even our sins could keep him from loving us. Not even the high cost of the cross could keep him from redeeming us. If we are the apple of his eye, then we should have eyes only for him.

Verse four says, "You shall not make for yourself an idol." Love means that you accept the one you love for who he or she is. You don't try to recreate that person into the image of what you want them to be. In the same way, you accept and worship God for exactly who he is. Remember, God loves you just the way you are. He is remaking you, but only to be like the person you were intended to be in Eden.

Verse seven says, "You shall not misuse the name of the LORD your God." If you love someone, you will treat that person with a sense of awe and reverence. You won't drag his or her name through the mud. You won't play games with that person's dignity or worth. God never speaks of you except with the most exalted of terms: "saint" and "beloved" and "chosen" along with a thousand other endearing names. In the same way, we should exalt his name and reverence his person.

Verse eight says, "Remember the Sabbath day by keeping it holy." If you love someone, you will want to spend quality time with that person. You will put your loved one first in your priorities. Is there any more precious gift to give anyone than your time? Remember, he is there all the time waiting for you. He delights in spending time with you. Do you delight in time alone with him?

The next six commandments tell you how to love your neighbor as yourself. The fifth commandment in verse twelve begins with the first neighbors we ever had: "Honor your mother and father." Our world is falling apart because parents and children do not love and honor each other. Those who haven't learned how to honor their families of origin will struggle all the days of their lives. Imagine how differently her life would have turned out, if only Norma Jean had started life in a loving family where everyone was honored.

Verse thirteen says, "You shall not murder." Verse fourteen says, "You shall not commit adultery." Verse fifteen says, "You shall not steal." Verse sixteen says, "You shall not give false testimony against your neighbor." Verse seventeen says "You shall not covet..." anything that belongs to your neighbor. Imagine the paradise this would be, if only we could love each other like this!

When Moses brought these commandments down from Sinai, it changed the history of the world. The best that we are in Western Civilization is because these laws have shown us how we should love. And yet, the worst things have happened because fallen people have not kept these laws of love.

4. THE LAW OF LOVE WILL BREAK OUR HEARTS

When Moses told the people about the Laws, they were scared. In Exodus 20:19, they cried out to Moses, "Speak to us yourself and we will listen. But do not have God speak to us or we will die." Most folks see the Commandments as fearful and burdensome.

Moses tries to calm their fears in verse twenty, "Do not be afraid, God has come to test you, so the fear of the Lord will be with you to keep you from sinning." Moses gives no comfort with those words. If we had been there at Mt. Sinai, we would have responded, "God has come to test us? Is that supposed to make us feel better?" We know that God doesn't grade on the curve.

He expects nothing less than perfection—a score of a hundred percent alone gives a passing grade

Moses says, "...the fear of the Lord will keep you from sinning." Again, we might respond, "Fear has never kept us from sinning." Fear and guilt are poor motives for doing what's right. They almost never produce any kind of righteousness. Moses no sooner goes back up the mountain to talk to God before the people begin to build a golden calf. In one fell swoop, they basically break all ten of the commandments.

When we realize the requirements involved in loving God with all our heart, soul, and mind, and then loving our neighbors as ourselves, we are doomed from the beginning. Mere mortals will never pass this severe test of love.

5. GRACE TRANSFORMS THOSE LOVED IN BROKENNESS

In Exodus 20:23, God again reminds Moses, "Do not make any gods to be alongside me." Within days they will erect the gold calf. But thank God for verse twenty-four: "Make an altar of earth for me and sacrifice on it your burnt offerings..."

This mound of earth is a picture of that mound of rock outside Jerusalem. Their burnt offerings are a picture of the lamb who will be crucified on it as the ultimate offering to God for our sins. Every one of us has denied God and destroyed our neighbors in the pursuit of the idols of our own making. The purpose of the Law of Love is to show us that we can't love in our own strength. The Law is good, but we aren't. The Law is designed to bring us to the end of ourselves and drive us to Jesus.

Jesus says in Matthew 5:3, "Blessed are the poor in spirit for theirs is the kingdom of heaven." When we are broken by the Law, and stand guilty before golden calves that have given us nothing in return for our idolatry, there is another altar over there: a mound of earth on which our Savior hangs crucified. He cries out, "Though you haven't loved me, I have always loved you." When we grasp those words and run into his stretched out arms, we will never be lonely again.

DESERT REFLECTIONS

The desert is the loneliest place on earth. If loneliness is a desert, then the whole world is a desert. The American sociologist and novelist, Thomas Wolfe writes, "Loneliness is the inevitable fact of human existence." After an audience with Queen Victoria, Alfred Lord Tennyson observed, "Sitting up there all alone in her majesty, she was after all just another lonely old woman." Tennyson could have been talking about most folks, maybe even you.

Roy Orbison asked a question in one of his hit songs: "Are you lonely tonight?" If so, you are crossing one of the most painful deserts of all. Marilyn Monroe was the toast of Hollywood and the object of fantasy for millions. She plowed through a succession of barren and broken relationships. Even her friend, actor Peter Lawford hung up on her in her greatest hour of need. Loneliness is the cruelest desert of all. It drove Norma Jean Mortensen to commit suicide.

But loneliness can be a tribulation that transforms your life. Remember, the dangling telephone? When no one else will answer, God is always waiting on the other end of the line. He has already called you, and is waiting patiently for you to pick up the phone. Will you come to him and be embraced by his love?

IDOLATRY

DESERT 11

"It is the normal state of the human heart to build its identity in something beside God."

Sorën Kierkegaard

Little Howie was almost deaf. After classmates made fun of him, he threw away his hearing aids. As a result, he lived with an incessant ringing in his ears. It nearly drove him insane, and then filled him with rage—especially when God didn't answer his desperate prayers. So Howie developed an implacable hatred of all things religious. By the time he was a teenager, his credo was set for life: if you can't depend on God for help, you have to become your own god.

Early on, Howie fell under the spell of his hypochondriac mother. Her paranoia of the bacteria that bred in the hot damp ness of Houston, Texas drove her to shield him from anyone or anything that might carry germs. If he got the slightest sniffle, she rushed him to the doctor. In the end, this paranoia would turn him into the world's most famous recluse.

As a teen, Howie was sent off to school in the dry climate of rural Southern California. There he discovered the two loves of his life: Hollywood and aviation. Lost in the magic of a movie, he forgot the ringing in his ears. Soaring high in an airplane, it stopped altogether.

He was only seventeen when his mother and father died, making him an instant multi-millionaire. He boasted to friends, "I'm bigger and richer than God." He set out to become the king of Hollywood, producing a string of movies— including two nominated for Oscars. He also got hooked on the drugs and depravities of Tinseltown and came down with incurable syphilis.

Howie also set his sights on becoming the king of the air. He built the H-1 Racer, the fastest airplane in history. In September of 1935, he flew to Paris in half the time it had taken Charles Lindberg, shattering all speed records. Then he stunned everyone by flying around the world in three days. He parlayed his father's business into the biggest supplier of parts and weapons for the Air Force and Navy. Along the way he founded TWA and became a household name as Howard Hughes, the first multi-billionaire in history. He bragged that he was not only richer than God, he was more powerful.

His bravado hid the fact that his syphilis was spreading. His old paranoia of germs returned with a vengeance. He moved to Las Vegas for the clean desert air. He bought the Desert Inn

Hotel and Casino and turned the top floor into his private sanctuary. There he lived like a hermit in a sanitary bubble. Then his agents bought up casinos surrounding the Desert Inn to extend his perimeter of control.

When he feared that testing nuclear weapons in Nevada might expose him to radiation, he spent millions bribing Lyndon Johnson, and later Richard Nixon, to stop the tests. When he suspected a Communist plot to unleash biological warfare on America, he funneled millions to the CIA for clandestine operations. Howard Hughes was becoming the world's ultimate control freak.

He got to the point where he was downing bottlefuls of medicine every day. Green peas were the only food he ate. Then he worried that he could choke to death on them. So he had each pea measured to make sure it was small enough. A barber came in once a year to cut his hair and fingernails. He kept a team of doctors on full alert, refused to wear clothes lest they hid germs, and walked around in Kleenex boxes for shoes. He never touched anything unless he was holding a paper towel in his hand. If a flu or cold epidemic hit the area where he was staying, he jetted off to another part of the world.

Around his 70th birthday, he fell into a coma. He was rushed by jet to Houston, but on August 5, 1976 he died in transit. He was worth four billion dollars, but his 6'4" frame had been reduced to ninety pounds. His body was covered in filth, his hair and beard were tangled and rancid, his fingernails looked like claws, and his arms were riddled with holes. X-rays showed broken needles lodged under his skin. The autopsy revealed that he died of renal failure and his brain was eaten by syphilis. His body was so unrecognizable that the FBI took fingerprints to prove it was really Howard Hughes.

When he was 17 years old, Howie vowed that he would be his own god. As a billionaire, he tried to control his universe. But the golden boy, who spent millions to isolate himself from germs, died ravaged by disease.

His tragic end screams a warning to idol makers: the golden calves we create to serve us will become our slave masters. We think they will carry us through life's difficulties. Instead, we will carry them until they break our backs, hearts, and lives. If Howie could come back, he would warn us to heed well the 11th principle of the Exodus journey:

THE GODS OF YOUR MAKING WEIGH YOU DOWN, BUT THE GOD WHO MADE YOU LIFTS YOU UP.

Remember where we are as we enter the thirty-second chapter of Exodus. The Israelites are camped at the base of Mt. Sinai. God has stepped out of heaven to sit atop that mountain. Nothing ever stays the same when God touches it. Sinai shakes and thunders, its top blackened by the LORD who is a consuming fire. Massive clouds hide God's glory, but dazzling light still flashes through in a pyrotechnic display of sound and fury that inspires fear and awe below.

A trembling Moses slowly climbs up that mountainside until he disappears into fiery clouds. Now the wait begins. Anxious hours turn into fretful days, which drag on into weeks. Finally, those below give up hope. Maybe this fearsome God has consumed Moses. You get a sense that an eerie silence has descended on Sinai. The people must wonder, "Has the God of Moses left too?"

I AM has an exasperating way of showing up, only to disappear. He speaks and then is silent. His presence is palpable and then we no longer feel it. He feeds us manna in the desert only to lead us into the Valley of the Shadow of Death. He prospers the wicked and allows the righteous to suffer. About the time we get our doctrinal formulas down pat, he throws a curve ball. In Romans 11:23&24, St. Paul captures the frustration of trying to solve the mystery of God:

"Oh, the depths of the riches of the wisdom and knowledge of God! How unsearchable his judgments, and his paths beyond tracing out! Who has known the mind of the Lord?"

Contemporary theologian Alex Burroughs cuts to the heart of idolatry: "Everyone wants God to take them just as they are; but no one wants to take God just as he is." The Israelites decide that God is too hot to handle. They need a manageable god. They need one who is relevant to what they are facing today: desolate deserts and enemy nations that will swallow them alive. They need a god tailor-made for their immediate crisis.

Beware of the subtle trap in making God and religion relevant. John Calvin wrote, "The most dangerous idols are the ones we form in our minds." We are too often tempted to reshape God and his religion to attract our culture, to address our felt needs, and to conform to our tastes and traditions. Again Alex Burroughs writes,

"Modern Evangelicals in particular stumble headlong into idolatry by spending too much time examining their own personal experience, trying to make sure God belongs to them—and less time examining the Scriptures to make sure they belong to him."

The frightened Israelites run to Moses' brother Aaron, the high priest of Israel, with a demand in Exodus 32:1, "Come, make us gods who will go before us." How often in history have God's people pressured their spiritual leaders to reshape theology to conform to their felt needs? Parishioners demand that their pastors preach sermons to tickle their ears, conduct worship services to please their tastes, and manufacture programs to keep them happy. Aaron, like too many clergy, becomes a people-pleaser rather than a God-server. It leads him to compromise his high calling. God help the flock when shepherds let the sheep set the direction for the journey!

Aaron answers in Exodus 32:2, "Take off the gold earrings that your wives, sons, and daughters are wearing and bring them to me." Exodus 32:4 says, "He took what they handed him and made it into an idol cast into the shape of a calf, fashioned with a tool."

Shame on Aaron! When the shepherd fleeces gold from the sheep in the name of advancing faith, watch out. When he crafts a god who will please the people rather than a people who will please their God, he has turned true religion into idolatry. Is there a hotter place in hell than that reserved for pastors who keep their jobs by compromising God's truth?

Later, Aaron will give the flimsiest of excuses, recorded in verse 24: "Then they gave me the gold, and I threw it into the fire, and out came this calf!" That calf didn't just pop out. Aaron carefully crafted that idol. The Hebrew should be translated bull. It is the diminutive of bull, so it is literally "a little gold bull."

The bull was the Egyptian god of power. Bulls are strong

and potent. They snort and paw the ground. When they charge, the earth shakes under their fury. They dominate the herd. What the Israelites want is a bull god who will go before them and strike fear in the hearts of their enemies. Pastor Aaron has given his parishioners a god who is relevant to their immediate felt need, and they go away happy. Isn't that what most folks want from their church?

But why is it a small bull? When he finishes crafting his masterpiece, he says in Exodus 32:4, "These are your gods O Israel, who brought you up out of Egypt." But he knows that this golden bull cannot carry the people on his back. Contrast this idol to what God said earlier in Exodus 19:4: "I carried you on eagles' wings and brought you up myself." But not even Aaron can craft a god who can carry 3.6 million people on its back. This god will not "...go up before them..." They will have to carry it on their backs. So it can't be too heavy. Is there anything worse than a preacher whose message is too heavy? We like our religion light, manageable, and convenient. So the bull is small because Aaron is a very practical pastor—the sort we all want.

What is idolatry? It is the invention of people who don't want to take God as he is. So they change the words of the creation story from "God created man in his image" to "man recreated God in his image."

When Moses first asked God his name, he replied, "I AM." R.C. Sproul says that God is saying, "I AM who I AM, not who you want me to be, or wish I would be, or conceive me to be, or feel me to be, or make me to be." Scotty Smith says, "An idol is anything that we look to for deliverance in the place of Jesus and his grace." Why are the gold bulls of our own making so devastating?

1. IDOLATRY SWAPS THE BEST FOR THE GOOD

There are lots of good things in this world. But only One can claim the title, "The Very Best." The first of the Ten Commandments says, "You shall have no other gods before me." Gold jewelry is beautiful. Bulls are necessary if you want a herd of cattle. Statues can be wonderful works of art, and Aaron must have been a good artist. But when the good becomes the object of our worship, we sold our lives cheaply for that which is less than the Best. St. Augustine wrote, "Idolatry is worshipping anything that ought to be used or using anything that ought to be worshipped."

Understand this: Golden calves don't just jump out of fires. Aaron lied when he offered that lame excuse. Remember the warning of John Calvin: "The most dangerous idols are the ones we form in our minds." The idols we craft are an extension of bad thinking. The truth is: that bull jumped out of Aaron's mind, not the fire.

Notice again what motivated the people's desire for an idol in Exodus 32:1: "As for this fellow Moses who brought us up out of Egypt, we don't know what has happened to him." Do you see the lie? It wasn't Moses who brought them out of Egypt. Moses was just an instrument in the hand of God. Moses was great only because the presence and power of God was on him. Moses was a good pastor, certainly better than Aaron. But God wasn't dependent on Moses. It is always foolish for God's people to put their trust in a pastor or his gifts. Do you see the trap in such thinking? Once God's people put their trust in a good man, it is only a short step to putting it in a golden bull.

That's why idolatry is the one sin, and the mother of all others. In Romans 1:15, Paul writes, "The wrath of God is being

revealed from heaven against all the godlessness and wicked-
ness of man who suppress the truth..." He goes on to tell us the
truth they suppress: God alone is our Creator, and he alone is to
be worshipped. Then he tells us the one sin that is the mother
of all other sins: "They exchanged the glory of the immortal
God for images made to look like mortal man and birds and
animals and reptiles." (Romans 1:24) In short, people worship
creation rather than the Creator.

St. Paul goes on in the rest of the first chapter of Romans
to tell us that God's wrath is revealed in that he gives us over to
all manner of sins: adultery, sexual perversions, strife, deceit,
murder, gossip, arrogance, ad infinitum ad nauseum. But there
is only one sin that matters; that which gives birth to all the
others: we chose to put our trust in created things rather than
the Creator. It was that way in the beginning. Adam and Eve
chose "the tree of the knowledge of good and evil" to give them
wisdom, pleasure, and beauty rather than the God who created
the tree. Everything he created is good, and has been given to
us for our enjoyment. Thank God for good leaders like Moses.
But when the good becomes the substitute for the One who
alone is best, we have sold our lives for a poor bargain that will
break our hearts in the end.

2. IDOLATRY SUBSTITUTES GIFTS FOR THE GIVER

Moses was a gift from God. In Ephesians 4:11, St. Paul tells
us that pastors and teachers are a gift from God to equip his
people. The jewelry those Israelites wore was also a gift from
God. On their way out of Egypt, God moved the hearts of the
Egyptians to give these ex-slaves gold, silver, and precious jewelry. It is ironic that the gifts of God should become the stuff

of idolatry. They looked to the prophet God had given them as their Savior. They took the jewelry God had given to make them beautiful and turned it into the ugliness of a bull god.

Thirty-five hundred years have come and gone, yet God's people do the same today. God gives us wealth, and we turn it into the basis of our security. He gives knowledge, and it becomes the source of our pride. He gives spiritual gifts, and we use them to elevate ourselves in the church. He gives wonderful traditions, and we hold on to them as if they were sacred. He gives the gift of faith, and then we think that it was our faith rather than our Lord that saw us through.

3. IDOLATRY SUBSTITUTES PERMANENT FOR IMMEDIATE

The people rushed to Aaron in panic. Look at their two concerns in verse one: "We don't know what happened to Moses." and "Who will lead us the rest of the way?" The tagline of a supermarket tabloid says, "Inquiring minds want to know!" From the time we were two year olds, we bugged our parents with that incessant, "Why?" It is a human failing as old as Adam and Eve eating the forbidden fruit from the Tree of the Knowledge of Good and Evil so that they could know the unknowable.

Hebrews 11:1 says that "...faith is the evidence of things not seen." But most of us live by sight, not faith. We need to see, touch, taste, and feel. Moses is gone from sight, and the God of Israel wraps himself in clouds. We ask "Why?" and he remains silent. We wait for a sign, and he gives none. We beg him to come and he stays away. So we make an idol. It has a sense of immediacy. We can see and touch it. We reduce the mysteries of God to pat formulas. We never stop to think that a god who can fit neatly into our finite minds, and is small enough to be seen by our eyes, is very tiny indeed.

And there is that other propensity of humankind: we are always in a hurry. Do you hear the silent scream of the Israelites: "We've waited at Mt. Sinai long enough. The clock is ticking. Let's move on out to the Promised Land." But God doesn't operate on our schedule. He is infuriatingly slow. So we jump the gun, and take the shortcut. Panic is the mother of idolatry. How many of us have sold our future by sacrificing the permanent on the altar of the immediate?

4. IDOLATRY SUBSTITUTES MAJESTY FOR MANAGEABLE

The God who meets them at Mt. Sinai is awesome to behold. Such majesty inspires terror. Postmodern Evangelicals have reduced God to the feel-good paternalistic grandfather who pats us on the head and says, "I hope you all have a good time today." Contemporary theologian, Michael Horton says, "Too many preachers today have turned their Sunday morning services into a caricature of the Dr. Phil Show, presenting a Jesus Christ who is a therapeutic life coach rather than a Living Savior that people desperately need."

But the God of Sinai is a Living God. And Hebrews 10:31 says, "It is a dreadful thing to fall into the hands of a Living God." He is unmanageable and unpredictable. He leads you where you don't want to go, and demands of you that which you don't want to do. He is never at our beck and call. He disappears when we need him most and appears again at the most inconvenient times. But the golden bull offers a solution to this unmanageable majesty of the God who insists on being Sovereign:

He is convenient in that we can take him out when we need

him, and store him away in a box when it suits our purposes.

He is changeable. Because he is gold, we can melt him down again and make him to become whatever we need him to be when a new set of circumstances arise. He can be a bird, snake, lion, or crucifix. He becomes a god for all seasons.

He is portable. We don't have to wait on him. If we want to leave Mt. Sinai, we can just hoist the bull up on poles and carry him out ahead of us. If we want to stop anywhere along the way, we can just put him down on the altar we build.

However, a god small enough to be manageable is unequal to the job when a major crisis arises. Then only an infinitely wise, strong, merciful, and holy God will do. Howard Hughes found out that all the money in the world couldn't build a bubble that would keep out the tiniest germs, or stop the tide of disease that ravaged his body. We can't have it both ways: either we will have a majestic God who is unmanageable or manageable gods that are not majestic.

5. IDOLATRY DEGRADES IDOLATERS

God made people in his image. We are best when we are like him, and we are most like him when we worship him. St. Paul wrote in 2 Corinthians 4:18, "And we, who with unveiled faces all reflect the Lord's glory, are being transformed into his likeness with ever-increasing glory..." There is an inviolate principle of life: we become like the God or gods that we worship. Look at what happens when they begin to worship that bull. Exodus 32:25 says,

> "Moses saw that the people were running wild and that
> Aaron had let them get out of control and so become a

laughingstock to their enemies."

When people worship a bull they become like a bull. The Hebrew words used to describe their actions speak of debauchery. Bulls are beasts of unbridled passions, and so were these idolaters. Bulls live to eat, procreate, and fight. And that's what the Israelites were doing. As postmodern people turn increasingly away from the God of the Bible, we should not be surprised at the level of depravity, debauchery and deception that seeps into every area of our culture. The idols we create always destroy our dignity. In the end, Howard Hughes became a bag-o-bones perforated with hypodermic needles. Life is full of warnings about the danger of idolatry.

So how do we respond to idolatry? Moses ripped into Aaron, and then he tore the idol down. He ground it into powder, mixed it with water and then made the people drink it. It was bitter medicine to swallow. It is never pleasant to ingest the truth.

The Bible calls this bitter gall repentance. It is always the first step to salvation, or coming back from backsliding away from God. Repentance is seeing yourself and your sin with the same eyes that God sees you and your actions. When you see with his eyes, it will break your heart in the same way that it breaks his heart. When the bitter medicine of repentance does its restorative work, you will want to turn away from your puny gods and run into the arms of his majesty.

DESERT REFLECTIONS

Howard Hughes grew up in a religious home. But when his childhood years turned into a desert crossing, he became embittered. He turned away from his Creator and tried to control creation so that it would promote his interests. Most of us are like Howard Hughes. The only difference is that he had the towering genius and massive fortune to take his idolatry into the stratosphere.

Howard Hughes stands as mute testimony to the fallacy of idolatry. Rather than embracing the desert crossing, he tried to build a painless paradise. In the end, he was as ravaged as any human being who ever crawled on hands and knees out of a desert.

Have you remade God in your own image? You have probably already discovered the sad truth: nothing of this creation has ever been able to stand up against life's stresses. Only the infinite and transcendent Creator is equal to the task.

It's not pleasant to ground your idols into powder and drink the bitter medicine of repentance. There is forgiveness, but you must crush your idols. Not one of them can remain. The journey to your Promised Land is too difficult for you to carry idols that can't get you there. They will only wear you down in the desert. So let the LORD pick you up and carry you all the way home.

BETRAYAL

DESERT 12

"One should rather die than be betrayed. There is no deceit in death. It delivers precisely what it has promised. Betrayal though is the willful slaughter of hope."
Steven Dietz

Betrayal rips out your guts. I first felt its piercing pain after my mother abandoned me when I was six years old. That betrayal was like a splinter of glass that worked its way deep into my heart. I fantasized that she would come back, but she never did.

At nine years of age, I dared hope again. My foster parents promised to adopt me. He took me fishing and told me he would love me forever. But, when she gave birth to their child, I was no longer his little boy. A few weeks later, a welfare worker showed up while he was at work and I was carted off to another foster home. I didn't even get to say goodbye to the man who promised to love me forever. I never saw him again.

The English writer John LeCarre wrote, "Betrayal can only happen if you love." Years ago a partner in ministry gave me a beautiful card in which he spoke of friendship and vowed his commitment. He hugged me and said, "I love you brother." He had already set in motion a plot to destroy my ministry. I viscerally felt the stabbing pain that others have felt. Jesus to Judas: "Do you betray me with a kiss?" St. Paul in prison: "Demus for the love of this world has left me." Julius Caesar to one of his assassins: "Et tu Brute?"

Surely Moses must have felt the back stab of betrayal. He had given his life to liberate his people. He had risked everything to go up Mt. Sinai. He knew that it is a dreadful thing to fall into the hands of a Living God. Yet he walked right into the blazing furnace of God's glory to receive the Law for their good. Never did a pastor love his people more than Moses loved them. But they betrayed that love. Imagine the pain that pierced his heart when God said in Exodus 32:7&8,

"Go down, because your people, whom you brought up out of Egypt, have become corrupt. They have been quick to turn away from what I commanded them and have made themselves an idol cast in the shape of a calf. They have bowed down to it and sacrificed to it and have said, 'These are your gods, O Israel, who brought you up out of Egypt.'"

Betrayal is always devastating. But, when those you love most betray your trust, the pain is always worse. Moses would agree with a wry comment made by Benjamin Franklin: "God defend me from my friends; from my enemies I can defend myself." We've all experienced the pain that Moses felt on Mt. Sinai. Each of our storehouses is filled with unwanted memories: promises broken, hopes gone awry, dreams dashed, trust betrayed, and friendships lost. Each of us has been betrayed. Worse, we have all betrayed others. We can say "amen" to Sigmund Freud's famous observation: "Betrayal oozes out of every pore of our being."

Here's the drama at Mt. Sinai: how will Moses respond to his betrayal? That's the challenge for all of us who are betrayed. There's no denying it: betrayal is a desolate desert. But here's the question: will we let it paralyze us, embitter us, or cause us to focus inwardly on hurts rather than look onward in hope? Betrayal can transform us into the likeness of our Lord if we can grasp this principle:

OUR HEART'S CONDITION IS MEASURED BEST WHEN IT IS BREAKING MOST.

When we give our heart to others, we put them in a position to break it. The Irish poet Oscar Wilde wrote, "Each man kills the thing he loves most." If our heart is broken enough, we will be tempted to seal it in a protective covering. Tennessee Williams penned these words: "If we are going to survive, we have to distrust each other. It's our only defense against betrayal." When a wife discovered that her husband had been unfaithful to her, she spurned his pleading for forgiveness with these words:

"The day you betrayed my trust was the day I lost all trust in you, I believed that you would take care of my heart and that's why I gave it to you. Well, I'm taking it back today. I'll never give you another chance to break it again."

People ask how I managed to overcome the betrayals in my childhood to still give my heart away. What's the secret of turning wounded yesterdays into a healthy today? By God's grace I have learned to put into practice Moses' attitudes and actions in the thirty-second chapter of Exodus. Here's how Moses overcame a broken heart:

1. DON'T MAKE IT PERSONAL; IT'S BIGGER THAN YOU

When people betray us, we often personalize it. We make it all about us. We obsess about the way we've been hurt. We focus on what needs to be done to make us feel better. It is our fallen nature to be self-focused.

Nothing illustrates this better than a line from the movie, Beaches. Bette Midler plays a self-obsessed drama queen. In one scene, she talks incessantly about herself. Finally she says to her friend, "Enough talk about me. Let's talk about you. What do you think about me?" We laugh because we see too much of ourselves in Bette Midler's character.

If people aren't friendly, we think, "Is there something wrong with me?" instead of, "I wonder if they're okay?" When others hurt us, we fixate on our wounds rather than their pain that caused them to lash out at us.

When someone else is getting all the attention or getting blessings that we wish were ours, we think, "What about me?" Maybe that's why one of my favorite movies is, "What About

Bob?" But it's never about Bob. Neither is it about Moses. Sure, he feels betrayed. But Moses sees immediately that making and worshiping the golden calf is first and foremost about God's glory, and not their betrayal of his leadership.

They have betrayed God by reducing his glory to that of a little golden bull. They have denied his grace by worshipping the works of their own hands. They have cheapened a blood sacrifice, intending to prefigure the crucifixion of Christ, by sprinkling it on the altar of an idol. They have also trashed God's goodness by praising their bull god as the one who brought them up out of Egypt.

Their sins may have wounded Moses, but they really grieved God. Sins we commit against people are always sins against God first. When people betray you, they are wounding your God. Your first focus should always be upward in agony for the grieving heart of God, not inward to your own grieving heart.

Because this betrayal is a slap in God's face, it puts the betrayers in mortal danger. God will not be mocked. We will always reap what we sow. The LORD says of them in Exodus 32:7, "They have become corrupt." He adds in verse nine, "They are a stiff-necked people." He concludes in verse ten, "Now leave me alone so that my anger may burn against them and I may destroy them."

If we grasped what it means for sinners to fall into the hands of an angry God, we would be petrified for them. Instead of fixating on his own pain, Jesus focused on the terrible wrath that would fall on those who crucified him. So he cried out for those who had betrayed him, "Father, forgive them..." When people betray us, it's their problem and not ours. Joseph Conrad wrote, "They talk about a man betraying his country, his friends, his sweetheart. But, first of all, a man must betray his own conscience."

Swiss Psychiatrist Henri Nouwen wrote, "Hurting people hurt people." Betrayal is always bigger than our personal hurt. That's why we need to look upward with concern for the God who has been betrayed, and outward in concern for the danger of the betrayer, before we look inward at the wounds of our betrayal.

2. TURN YOUR BITTERNESS INTO BETTERNESS

After an angry God says that he will destroy the Israelites, he cuts a deal with Moses at the end of Exodus 32:10. "Then I will make you into a great nation."

God is offering Moses the same deal he cut with Abraham 500 years before. He'll wipe the slate clean, and then start over with Moses as the father of a new covenant people. If Moses was consumed with bitterness, he might have jumped at this offer. How many times have some of us wished that God would kill the people who have broken our hearts (or at least hit them with a plague or two?)

As you will see in a moment, God never intended to destroy those idolaters. He was pushing Moses to be as gracious and faithful as he was. We can learn so much from that wounded pastor's response in verse eleven: "But Moses sought the favor of the LORD his God..." The Hebrew word for favor is literally grace. The word sought means to pursue something with all the passion you possess. Moses is pulling out all the stops, wrestling with his LORD to be a God of grace. Immediately, we see another key to getting over the wounds of betrayal: we have to fight through pain to gain God's heart.

Remember, this is not about Moses. It is first and foremost

about God's glory. Moses argues that God would deny his very character if he destroyed the nation of Israel. He argues in Exodus 32:12, "Why should the Egyptians say, 'It was with an evil intent that he brought them out to kill them in the mountains...'" Moses can't stand the thought that pagan nations would dismiss his God as evil or rash. He goes on in verse thirteen, "Remember your servants Abraham, Isaac, and Israel to whom you swore by your own self..." He cannot stand that his God would be laughed at as a covenant breaker.

He also pleads for the very people who betrayed him because it's also about the sinner's salvation. He cries out in Exodus 32:12, "Turn away your fierce anger; relent and do not bring disaster on your people." In Moses' pleading with God on Mt. Sinai, we hear an echo from Mt. Calvary: "Father, forgive them..." Billy Graham once observed, "When we sin against God or others, we want mercy. When others sin against us we want justice." It's hard to plead for mercy for those who wound us. But those who possess the heart of Jesus will do exactly that!

Jesus said, "Blessed are the merciful for they will be shown mercy." (Matthew 5:7) Moses could have curled up in a ball of bitterness. That's what some of us have done. But he plowed through his own bitterness, by pleading for mercy for those who betrayed God and him. Because Moses was merciful, God showed mercy to him and his idolatrous people. Exodus 32:14 says,

"Then the Lord relented and did not bring on his people the disaster he had threatened."

Moses turned his bitterness into their betterness. I remember when I couldn't shake the bitterness I felt toward some folks who had betrayed me. I walked in the mountains of a Caribbean island, weeping in anguish. Deep inside, I rebelled at forgiving them. The next day, while browsing through a bookstore, I ran across R.T. Kendall's book, Total Forgiveness. He said, "You have not truly forgiven those who hurt you until you actively pray for God to bless them."

That's what Moses did. Jesus says in Matthew 5:44, "Love your enemies and pray for those who persecute you." John Calvin writes, "This kind of mercy is exceedingly difficult." The Fourth Century Church Father John Chrysostom said, "It is the very highest summit of self-control. It is to become like Jesus himself."

When I prayed for God to bless my betrayers, my bitterness began to lift. I would like to tell you that it never came back. But, when I least expect it, it still does. Total forgiveness is a long-term commitment. You need to practice it every day of your life until you die to the bitterness. It is never easy. But it takes away your resentment, blesses God, and makes others better.

3. TURN YOUR PAIN INTO PRODUCTIVITY

The first thing Moses did was to get his focus and feelings right. Then he took action to set things right. If we wait until the hurt goes away, we will never be any help to anyone else. To get our feelings right, we have to do right even when we don't feel right.

FACE IT HEAD ON AND SOON

Exodus 32:15 says, "Moses turned and went down the mountain with the two tablets of the Testimony in his hands..." Let's unpack that little verse. First, Moses turned away from the

God with whom he had been wrestling. When we are wounded we need to go to God first. Like Moses, we may even have to wrestle with him before we can get our head and heart in the right place. But there comes a time when we have to get up and go back and face the world that betrayed us. No one ever got healthier by hiding.

Secondly, he went down the mountain. It wasn't easy to go down. On the mountain, he basked in God's holy glory. Down below, the people are engaged in unspeakable depravities. He's going to have to confront them head on, and that's never pleasant. He will be putting his life on the line. But, when brothers and sisters are sinking into the quicksand of sin, we must go down into the muck and rescue them.

Thirdly, Moses went with the two tablets of the Testimony in his hands. The Bible hadn't been written yet. These two tablets of the Law were the only written Word that Moses had at his disposal. But he took it, because that was all he had on which to stand. We have so much more than Moses possessed: a whole Bible that gives us all the authority we need to deal with relationships gone awry.

Is there a broken relationship in your life? Ephesians 4:26&27 says, "Don't let the sun go down on your wrath, lest you give the devil a foothold." Time doesn't heal all wounds. It only makes them fester. If we don't act immediately, we give the devil a foothold. The only thing that heals wounds is medicine: cutting out the cancer of sin, the sting of confession and acid taste of repentance, then sewing up the wounds with words of grace, followed by applying the soothing salve of total forgiveness. We have to face it head on—the sooner, the better.

ACT WITH REASON, NOT RASHNESS

We should be glad that Moses took a few hours to get down that mountain. He had time to think things through. James 1:19&20 says, "Everyone should be quick to listen, slow to speak, and slow to become angry, for man's anger does not bring about the righteousness that God desires." In the silence of the walk, Moses formulated a redemptive strategy.

Step one: he threw down the tablets, shattering them. Exodus 32:19 says, "His anger burned..." It's not always wrong to show our anger. There are too many sweet saints trying to appease a politically correct culture. Sometimes we need to get viscerally and visibly angry in the face of evil. When Moses shatters those tablets, he is giving an object lesson by saying that they have broken God's heart along with the Law. In short, he is confronting them with the heinousness of their sin.

Step two: he destroyed the golden bull. We all have to topple the idols in our lives. Nothing or no one can come before God. Exodus 32:20 says that Moses grounded the idol up into powder, scattered it on the water, and made them drink it. This is bitter medicine. Commenting on Moses' actions, a well-known internist said that this would make people sick to their stomach, resulting in violent retching. We have to confront the awfulness of our sins, even though it makes us want to throw up.

Step three: He confronted Aaron in verse twenty-one: "What did these people do that you led them into such great sin?" Moses' confrontation was so severe that Aaron shrank back in terror. We might all want to pray that God would give us leaders who are not afraid to put the fear of God in people. Church discipline is a relic of a bygone past, and God's people have become impotent because of it.

Finally, Moses called the people to strap on swords and go

throughout the camp slaying those who refused to turn from this idolatry. A terrible slaughter followed. It offends our post-modern sensibilities. But Moses knew that he had to tear this idolatry out by its roots or it would spring up again to corrupt his people. By the end of the day, this great leader had restored order to the people of God. And so we are called to bring God's order to the disorder in our relationships. It's not easy to confront sin, and it has to be done with care and humility. But it must be done.

POINT TO THE CROSS

Exodus 32:30 says, "The next day Moses said to the people, 'You have committed a great sin. But now I will go up to the Lord; perhaps I can make atonement for your sin'" When he carries the sins of his people back up that mountain, we see Jesus carrying our sins on his back up another hill outside Jerusalem. On the Cross Jesus made atonement for our sins.

Notice Moses said, "Perhaps I can make atonement..." It is a wishful hope. The truth is: he can't make atonement. But, when he goes back up on Mt. Sinai, God gives him a plan that is recorded in the rest of Exodus, Numbers, Leviticus and Deuteronomy: a plan for a tabernacle, priests, sacrifices, washings, cleansings, dietary laws, and feast days. It's an exhausting plan, confusing to some of us. But in it, God is carving out a graphic picture of his Only Begotten Son who will come to carry his people's sins, shed his blood on the Cross, and make atonement for them. Only at the Cross is grace found, and total forgiveness possible. We must always go there together if we are to find peace.

INTERCEDE FOR THE BEST FOR YOUR BETRAYERS

In Exodus 32:32 Moses pleads, "But now, please forgive their sin—but if not, then blot me out of the book you have written." Catch your breath here. Moses is literally saying, "If you don't forgive them, then take my name out of the Book of Life." Jesus said, "If you don't forgive men their sins, your Father will not forgive your sins." (Matthew 6:15) Moses is saying the reverse to God: "If you don't forgive men their sins, then don't forgive my sins." He is holding God to the same standard that God holds us to.

This Moses is very clever. More than that, he has a great heart of mercy and grace. Indeed, it is not total forgiveness until you would do anything (even get yourself written out of the Book of Life) to see mercy and blessings poured out on those who have hurt you. Jesus prayed for his betrayers, "Father, forgive them for they know not what they do." Moses didn't have to go to hell to get his people forgiven, but Jesus did. Yet, isn't it great that Moses had the heart of Jesus? Do you have his heart?

LEAVE THE OUTCOME IN GOD'S HANDS

Moses didn't get everything for which he prayed. God answered him in Exodus 32:34, "However, when the time comes for me to punish, I will punish them for their sins." The Lord struck them with a horrific plague according to his schedule and will. That wasn't what Moses wanted to happen, but it pleased God to respond to their act of betrayal with a severe mercy.

Total forgiveness is to say what Jesus said on the Cross: "Father, into your hands I commit my spirit." He said almost the same thing the night before in Gethsemane: "Nevertheless, your will be done." When Moses brings the pains of his betrayal to the God of his comfort, he must trust God to deal perfectly with his wounds and to respond perfectly to the ones who wounded him.

Only when we can put our wounded hearts into the nail-scarred hands of the Great Physician can we also echo his cry from the Cross, "It is finished!" Finally, we can walk away from the bitterness of betrayal knowing that our Savior will handle it well. And, because the past is left behind, we can focus on the journey ahead.

DESERT REFLECTIONS

Betrayal turns life into a desert crossing. When Moses was forty, he was betrayed by his own rash impulses and murdered an Egyptian overseer. His own slave people betrayed him when they refused to follow him. His adopted grandfather, the Pharaoh of Egypt, betrayed him by declaring him a criminal and traitor. An avalanche of betrayals drove him into the harshness of his Sinai exile.

For Moses this was the desert of betrayal. But, in an ironic twist, his desert became his refuge from further betrayals. When God called him to return to Egypt, he fought to stay hidden in his desert.

Maybe betrayal has turned your life into a desert crossing. But the time has come for you to go back and face those who betrayed you, or fess up to those you have betrayed. At least, you must go back and open your life again to others who might betray you.

Remember, the desert is not a terminal place. It is a temporary crossing for a transformed future. You cannot get to your Promised Land without first going through a series of deserts, but neither can you enter your Promised Land without finally leaving the deserts behind.

Moses would face more betrayals and cross harsher deserts before his journey was over. His people, his own family, and even his own weaknesses would betray him. But, one day, he stood in transformed glory with Christ on the Mount of Transfiguration. And so will you, if only you will let betrayal transform rather than transfix your soul.

CRITICISM

DESERT 13

*"Criticism is a study by which men grow important and
formidable at very small expense...He whom nature has
made weak, and idleness keeps ignorant, may yet sup-
port his vanity by the name a critic."*

Samuel Johnson

Fifteen year-old Phoebe was one of the most popular girls
at South Hadley High. Within weeks after she emigrated with
her family from Ireland, she was dating the star of the football
team. A few months later she was going out with the most
popular senior in the school.

It's no wonder. Phoebe was a pretty girl with a Mona Lisa

smile. The Irish lilt to her voice made her even more irresistible. But it wasn't long before the teen queen bees at Hadley High were seething with jealousy and came after this Irish interloper with a vengeance that shocked America.

Their slander turned Phoebe into a social outcast. But that wasn't enough for these mean girls. They launched a relentless campaign of cyber bullying, flooding her email with hate speech. They twittered and texted ugly messages and called her cruel names on her Facebook. On January 14, 2010 a carload of mean girls drove along side her, screaming taunts and throwing bottles at her. She ran into her house, locked herself in her room, and hanged herself.

Her Massachusetts community was shocked that a young girl could be tormented to death right under their noses. Boston Globe columnist Kevin Cullen coined a new phrase when he said that the mean girls were guilty of cybercide. The District Attorney charged them with harassment, claiming that their bullying pushed Phoebe over the edge.

This cybercide spawned outrage across America. It has also sparked a legal debate: are people liable if their cyber bullying drives someone to commit suicide? The New York Times Bloggerhead interviewed Ann Althouse of the University of Wisconsin Law School. Ms. Althouse argues that criminalization of cyber bullying is a slippery slope:

> "If you commit murder, you can't say, 'That person made my life a living hell and I was driven to do it.' You are still guilty of murder. The fact that they made your life difficult doesn't change the fact that you did the killing. In the same way, if someone takes their own life, that person made the decision to kill them self. Though people may have made

life a living hell for the victim, they cannot be held legally liable for the decision of that person to commit suicide."

Ms. Althouse may be right when it comes to legal liability. But a question remains. It's as old as Cain's question in Genesis 4:9: "Am I my brother's keeper?" Even if my brothers and sisters are as fragile as Phoebe Prince, am I morally culpable for what my words drive them to do? Though I may not be liable before an earthly court, will I have to answer before heaven's bar?

The half-brother of Jesus wrote in James 3:8, "The tongue is a restless evil, full of deadly poison." Jesus talks about a man in hell who begs for a drop of water to soothe his pain. It's intriguing that he asks that it be placed on his tongue. Is Jesus saying that the body part, which torments others most on earth, will itself experience the most torment in hell?

The tongue is deadliest when criticizing. How many children have been warped by it? How many marriages have been ruined? How many careers have been lost? How many friendships destroyed? How many churches split? How many Phoebes driven over the edge?

The wisest man who ever lived said in Proverbs 18:21, "For the power of life and death are in the tongue." We are responsible for our words. Jesus warns us in Matthew 12:36, "But I tell you that men will have to give account on the day of judgment for every careless word they have spoken." Those mean girls at South Hadley High will stand before God and answer for Phoebe. But, each of us will also answer for our cruel and careless words.

We had better learn how to deal with this thing called criticism. Surely Moses knew the pain of criticism. He was bullied by it every day for forty years. Other than Jesus, no one ever handled it better than Moses. Criticism turns a garden into a desert. If we are going to keep from destroying others by our critical words, or not be debilitated by the criticism of others, we need to learn this principle:

CRITICISM MAY NOT BE AGREEABLE,
BUT IT IS NECESSARY
AS IT CALLS ATTENTION TO
AN UNHEALTHY STATE OF THINGS.

Take what happened in Hadley. The venom that spewed from the mean girls exposed their festering hearts. Phoebe's frantic cries for help revealed her fragile heart. But school officials dismissed the bullying as typical teenage stuff. Parents sloughed it off as "Kids will be kids." In reporting the tragedy, Time magazine asked, "Why didn't adults take action to avert the tragedy?" Indignant second-guessers across America asked the same question.

It's easy to judge the officials at South Hadley High for doing nothing. But the truth is: all of us listen to and spew verbal venom every day. From judging contestants on American Idol to screaming at referees to forwarding emails mocking our president's performance, criticizing others is a national pastime. From the water cooler at work to the coffee hour at church, we participate nonstop in whining and complaining.

Like the folks in Hadley, we don't even grasp the unhealthy state of things taking place right under our noses. So we need to evaluate how we deliver and receive criticism in order to measure our spiritual state. As we watch criticism swirl about

Moses, we get answers to three questions

1. HOW DO WE GIVE CONSTRUCTIVE CRITICISM?

Let's look at one of the original mean girls. Her name is Miriam. She's the older sister of Moses. And she is as jealous of him as the mean girls of South Hadley High were of Phoebe Prince. So she enlists Aaron in an attack against Moses. We read in Numbers 12:1&2,

"Miriam and Aaron began to talk against Moses because of his Cushite wife, for he had married a Cushite. 'Has the Lord spoken only through Moses?' they asked. 'Hasn't he also spoken through us?' And the Lord heard this."

It's a good thing that the Internet or Facebook hadn't been invented by 1400 BC, or this mean girl could have done some serious damage. As it was, only one thing matters and it is recorded at the end of Numbers 12:2: "And the Lord heard..." We are careless with our words, not even giving them a second thought. Ben Franklin said, "Any fool can criticize and complain, and most fools do." We shrug and say, "No harm, no foul." We even forget our words that wounded others. But God hears. Nothing we say is insignificant to him. And, he never forgets. So what are our takeaways?

WE NEED TO BE AWARE OF AN ADDICTION TO CRITICIZING

Miriam and Aaron were shaped in a culture of criticism. Three verbs are repeated with nauseating regularity to describe the Israelites throughout the Exodus: "grumbling, complaining and murmuring." You see it just a few verses before in Numbers 11:4-6:

"The rabble with them began to crave other food, and again the Israelites started wailing and said, 'If only we had meat to eat! We remember the fish we ate in Egypt at no cost— also the cucumbers, melons, leeks, onions and garlic. But now we have lost our appetite; we never see anything but this manna.'"

In 1 Corinthians 19:9&10 Rabbi Paul said that the paramount sin in Israeli history was complaining. When we study Jewish history, we see two reasons why the Israelites developed a culture of criticism. The same two reasons explain why people the world over are criticizers: 1) People who suffer the most can become the most critical. No people ever suffered more than the Jews. For 400 years they were slaves in Egypt. Having been abused, they distrusted authority. After years of deprivation, they became negative and fearful. After centuries of figuring that God had abandoned them, they found it difficult to trust him again.

A critical spirit became part of their collective psyche. We can't excuse the followers of Moses, but we should try to understand them. We should also watch out for ourselves when we go through tough times. Betrayal can make us bitter. Suffering may cause us to be skeptical. The abused often distrust those in authority. The poor resent the prosperous. Losers are jealous of winners. Bad times give birth to a critical spirit.

On the other end of the spectrum: 2) People who have been the most blessed can become the most critical. No folks were blessed more than these Jews. They walked through seas on dried land, drank from rivers flowing supernaturally from desert rocks, ate the bread of heaven, and witnessed spectacular miracles. Yet, the more these Israelites received, the more dissatisfied they became.

Beware if you are enjoying the good life. Prosperity breeds pomposity. Attractiveness spawns arrogance. Being in a superior position gives birth to a sense of superiority. Being served produces feelings of entitlement. Good times are a recipe for a critical spirit.

A 2010 issue of Business Week magazine presented a study from the British University of Leicester that ranked the world's happiest nations. Though America is the richest nation in history, it only ranked 23rd in contentment. Conversely, Zimbabwe, the poorest country on earth, ranked at the bottom of the 173 nations. The survey found that the wealthiest and poorest nations on earth both lacked contentment. Both ranked at the top when it came to complaints about life. Like Miriam and Aaron, we are prone to criticism. The first step to getting over it is to admit we are children of a culture of criticism. It is our nature to be critical. We have to fight to overcome it.

WE NEED TO BE UPFRONT IN OUR CRITICISMS

Notice a key word in Numbers 12:1: "Miriam and Aaron began to talk against Moses." They should have talked to or with Moses. Instead, they went behind his back and talked against him to others. They chose cheap gossip over godly confrontation. Jesus tells us in Matthew 18:15, "If your brother sins against you, go and show him his fault, just between the two of you." There is only one legitimate reason to criticize, and that is to help the other person get better.

Abraham Lincoln said, "He has a right to criticize who has a heart to help." Jesus is clear: "...go and show him his fault, just between the two of you." It is never helpful to show others his faults. It only corrupts them, and never helps the one we're talking about. Let's be frank: Gossip is the way of the coward.

WE NEED TO BE HONEST IN OUR CRITICISMS

What was Miriam and Aaron really upset about? Numbers 12:1 says they, "...began to talk against Moses because of his Cushite wife, for he had married a Cushite." The Hebrew sentence structure is very emphatic: they didn't like her because of her race. When Moses was a fugitive in the Sinai, he had married Zipporah, a woman of a nomadic tribe called Midianites. These descendants of Noah's son Cush had migrated to the Sinai from Africa. Zipporah was a black woman, and Miriam and Aaron were racists who resented this woman of color because she had married into their family.

But they had to mask their dirty little secret. After all, Miriam was a prophetess and Aaron was the High Priest. So they piously say in Numbers 12:2, "Has the Lord only spoken through Moses? Hasn't he also spoken through us?" They are saying, "Moses is hogging the limelight and not giving others the opportunity to use their spiritual gifts."

I can't tell you how often I've heard this criticism in the church. But Miriam and Aaron are blatantly dishonest. They are wrapping their racism in a pious protest. God's people are very skilled at putting a religious mask on their carnality. Be careful before you criticize others. You may be deceiving yourself even as you deceive others.

WE NEED TO BE GENTLE WITH OUR CRITICISMS

Miriam and Aaron were as brutal as the mean girls of South Hadley High. In Numbers 12:8, God rebuked them: "Were you not afraid to speak against my servant, Moses?" The Hebrew phrase has the sense of a no-holds-barred, frontal attack.

Miriam and Aaron were not only vicious, they were arrogant: "Hasn't God also spoken through us?" In other words, "Aren't our prophetic gifts as good as his?" God was quick to cut them down to size. In Numbers 12:6 he speaks to run-of-the-mill prophets with ordinary dreams and visions. But he said of Moses in verse eight: "With him I speak face to face, clearly and not in riddles; he sees the form of the Lord." In short, God was saying to Miriam and Aaron, "I know Moses. And you are no Moses."

In Galatians 6:1 St. Paul warns us, "Brothers, if someone is caught in sin, you who are spiritual should restore him gently. But watch yourself or you also may be tempted." Before you go criticize someone else: 1) make sure the other person is really in sin; 2) make sure you are truly spiritual; 3) rebuke with a gentle spirit; and 4) watch out for pride. Otherwise, keep it to yourself. Frank A. Clark writes, "Criticism, like the rain, should be gentle enough to nourish a man's growth without destroying his roots."

WE NEED TO BE CAREFUL WHEN WE CRITICIZE

In Numbers 12:8 God says, "Were you not afraid to speak against my servant Moses?" The key is "my servant." In Psalm 105:15 the LORD says, "Touch not my anointed." The anointed are those set apart by God to be in authority over us: parents, pastors, and princes. You may not always approve of what they do, but you are to pray for them and honor them because God put them in their positions.

We live in a culture where it is open season on everyone in authority. From comedians to radio talk hosts to the emails we forward, we take cheap shots at those whom God has placed over us. This doesn't mean that we can't disagree with our leaders, and even vote them out of office. But shouldn't we tread carefully when we criticize and trivialize people who have been placed there by God?

It was Winston Churchill who said, "Criticism may not be agreeable, but it is necessary. It fulfills the same function as pain in the human body. It calls attention to an unhealthy state of things." Sometimes the way we criticize others says more about us than the people we are criticizing.

2) HOW SHOULD WE RECEIVE CRITICISM?

Though the mean girls of South Hadley High revealed festering hearts through their ungodly criticism, Phoebe's response to criticism showed that her heart was fatally fragile. Moses' response to the bullying of Miriam and Aaron showed the greatness of his heart. Here's what we learn from it:

DON'T DEFEND YOURSELF

Notice the silence of Moses. He never responds to the criticism. 1) He knows that it goes with the territory. At first, Moses came unglued every time the people attacked him. But after thirty years of being criticized, he has finally made peace with being unpopular. Aristotle famously said, "If you want to avoid criticism you just have to do nothing, say nothing, and be nothing."

2) Years of criticism have shaped his character. He says nothing to defend himself, but God says in Numbers 12:3, "Now Moses was a very humble man, more humble than anyone else on the face of the earth." Moses wasn't always humble. When he was the Prince of Egypt, he killed a man in a fit of rage. Earlier in the desert crossing, he beat on a rock in a

fit of rage. But years later, he is the most humble man on the planet. What changed him? Maybe actor Paul Newman gives the best answer: "If you get enemies, you will get character."

3) He knew that only God's opinion really matters. Miriam and Aaron accused him of spiritual pride. But God said that he was the humblest man on earth. We worry too much about our reputations. Bill Gothard used to say in his Basic Youth Conflicts seminars, "Reputation is what other people say about you. Character is what God knows about you."

LISTEN FOR WHAT YOU CAN LEARN

If Moses didn't speak, we should assume that he listened. James 1:19 says, "Everyone should be quick to listen, slow to speak, and slow to become angry." It is not easy to listen to criticism, especially if it is delivered in a godless manner. We often use the bad way people criticize us as an excuse not to listen. The truth is: it's never easy to hear criticism, even if it's godly.

The famous writer and observer of human nature, Summerset Maugham put it this way: "People ask for criticism, but they only want praise." Remember our principle for crossing this particular desert: Criticism may not be agreeable, but it is necessary as it calls attention to an unhealthy state of things.

We might be tempted to protest, "But there was nothing wrong with Moses! Miriam and Aaron's criticism was bogus." But Moses still had to listen. Remember, what we learned on the desert of betrayal: it's not just about us. The criticism directed at us may be revealing more about the criticizer's problems than our own. Our concern should be their healing, not just our pain at being falsely accused.

GIVE TOTAL FORGIVENESS TO FALSE ACCUSERS

One of the reasons Moses can remain humble in the face of this vicious attack is that he trusts God to fight his battles for him. God will never stand by idly and watch his anointed take it on the chin. If you belong to God, you never have to defend yourself. Jesus said that you can even turn the other cheek.

God comes down hard on that mean girl, Miriam. Numbers 12:10 says that she was stricken with leprosy. But Moses takes no delight in God's judgment on the sister who viciously slandered him. He pleads in verse thirteen, "O God, please heal her." We may begrudgingly offer forgiveness to those who have wounded our hearts and destroyed our reputations, but we have not given total forgiveness until we pray for God to bless them. Until we can do that, we have not yet been transformed into the likeness of Christ who said, "Love your enemies and pray for those who persecute you that you may be sons of your Father in heaven." (Matthew 5:44&45)

3) HOW DOES GOD RESPOND TO GODLESS CRITICISM?

The answer is short and scary: with holy anger! Aaron and Miriam are brought before the Lord. Numbers 12:9 says, "The anger of the Lord burned against them, and he left them." The most terrible thing of all is for the Lord to leave us. In the Old Testament, when God left the temple, the word Ichabod was placed over it. Ichabod is a combination of Hebrew words, which literally means: "the glory has departed." How may churches have Ichabod written across their doors? How many Christians have it written across their hearts?

God's glory does not reside in the critic, faultfinder, complainer, whiner, gossip, or slanderer. In Proverbs 6:17-19, we are told that there are six things the Lord hates, but a seventh that he detests. What is the thing that he detests most? Proverbs 6:19 says, "...a man who stirs up dissension among brothers." That's what Miriam and Aaron did. God's glory can never be among his people when they are fighting amongst themselves.

When his glory departs, Miriam is covered with leprosy. Why isn't Aaron afflicted with the same disease? The only thing we might guess is that Miriam was the instigator of the attack on Moses. In Numbers 12:1, Miriam is mentioned before Aaron. In ancient Semitic writings a woman is never listed before the man in a sentence. Clearly, the writer is putting her in the dominant position to remind us that she was the mastermind in this coup against Moses.

Indeed, God's judgment is poetic in its perfection. Miriam resented the black woman's skin color, and now her skin is covered with white flakes of leprosy. She tried to push Zipporah out of the family, and now she is quarantined outside the camp. She attempted to shame Moses, but now she is an object of shame. She aimed to bring down Moses, and now she has been brought low. Indeed the words of Scripture have come true for Miriam and her brother Aaron: "Pride comes before a fall." Has anyone ever illustrated more graphically the modern proverb: What goes 'round comes 'round? The next time we set out to criticize someone, we might want to remember Miriam.

But God also heals with gracious mercy. God's punishment is severe but it isn't forever. In Numbers 12:14 he says,

"Confine her outside the camp seven days, and after that she can be brought back."

Why does she get to come back? What is our hope when we are under judgment for our careless and cruel tongues? It is in the fact that another also went outside the camp just like Miriam. Though he never said a cruel thing in his life, he was dragged outside the city and separated from God's people. He was taken to a pile of rocks in a garbage dump where lepers picked through trash. He was nailed to a cross, and covered with our shame. He literally became sin, as surely as Miriam became leprous. He was rejected like every Miriam who has ever come under the wrath of God for a careless tongue.

All of that he suffered so that Miriam and all the mean girls who ever tried to destroy others with their criticism might be redeemed and rejoin God's people. He was fatally wounded so that every Phoebe, whose fragile heart has been fatally wounded by critics, might find healing and restoration.

DESERT REFLECTIONS

Those days that Miriam stood outside the camp were devastating for this proud woman. She who had gossiped was now the object of everyone's gossip. But her soul needed this seven-day desert crossing. Without this tribulation, she might never find transformation. We should never despise the shame that leads to spiritual healing. During that terrible week, Aaron must have lived in fear that the hammer of God would fall on him too. It is a good thing for all of us to fear that God can still discipline us for our critical spirits and words.

Perhaps you are Miriam, or Aaron, or one of the mean folks who has made a desert for others. Maybe you are Phoebe or Moses whose life has been turned into a desert by mean folks. Only when you go outside the camp and grab hold of the One who suffered your sin and shame, will you be restored to God who forgets every cruel word you have ever said or suffered. Only at the Cross can you forgive others the same way.

FINISHING

DESERT 14

"When the game is over, both kings and pawns go back into the same box."

Italian Proverb

After an epic battle, the emperor was now the undisputed master of a vast subcontinent. Yet it was a hollow victory for Shah Jahan. His wife had just died in childbirth, and he was in utter despair.

For nineteen years the Princess of Persia had been his soul mate. Their passionate love affair was the stuff of storybook legend. In an age when Asian kings kept their women hidden away in harems, she was his chief advisor and confidant. She even rode by his side into battle. She also gave birth to thirteen of his children, and died delivering the fourteenth.

His grief was monumental. For eight days he locked himself in his private chambers, refusing to eat or drink. When those in the palace heard the animal moans and howling from behind his closed doors, they were sure that the Shah had gone mad. When he finally emerged, they gasped in horror. His raven black hair had turned snow white. He was now stooped over like an old man. In eight days he had shrunk noticeably in size.

He demanded that his millions of subjects join him in a year's mourning. A decree went out banning all popular music, public amusements, perfumes, cosmetics, jewelry, and brightly colored clothes. For the next year, those caught smiling, laughing, or engaged in any pleasure, were dragged before tribunals. Thousands were executed.

The Shah's sorrow had reduced his vast kingdom to the most desolate place on earth.

Then he turned his grief into a frenzy of activity. He imported the finest architects and craftsmen to build the greatest monument to love the world had ever seen—a magnificent mosque that would house the treasured remains of his departed wife.

More than 20,000 workers took 22 years to build it. Thousands of elephants dragged in the most precious stones and timbers from all over Asia. The mosque, together with its gardens and reflecting pools, covered 42 acres. It cost billions in today's dollars.

Centuries later, it remains one of the architectural marvels of history. It has been called the eighth wonder of the world. When the project was complete, the Shah ordered the architectural plans destroyed and the architects murdered so that they could never build anything to rival his magnificent memorial to his wife. Afterwards, the hands of the master craftsmen were cut off so they could never be used again.

Perhaps you have seen the monument that Shah Jahan erected to his wife, Mutaz Mahal—the breathtakingly beautiful Taj Mahal. The wife of a British officer once said, "I would gladly die tomorrow if some man loved me enough to put such a building over my grave." When he first saw the Taj Mahal, Indian poet Rabindranath Tagore wrote, "It is the one teardrop of grief that glistens spotlessly on the cheek of time forever."

You may have gazed in awe at the Taj Mahal, but do you know the secret that will never appear in a tourist guidebook? When Shah Jahan was visiting the work site, he tripped over a wooden box that had been carelessly left among the rubble. He angrily ordered it thrown away. The terrified workers tossed the box onto a garbage pile. Only later did they discover the horrific truth: that box contained the remains of the Shah's beloved wife, Mutaz Mahal. By then, it had disappeared forever.

At the center of this "eighth wonder of the world" is an ornate but empty tomb that perpetrates one of history's greatest frauds. And the remains of the woman for whom it was built lies buried amongst forgotten garbage.

The Taj Mahal stands as mute testimony to the tragedy of wasted life. Like Shah Jahan, we can give our energies to great endeavors. We might be motivated by the noblest of reasons. Millions may even admire our work for years after we die. Yet, like Shah Jahan's Taj Mahal, they may be a magnificent façade hiding an empty hoax.

Now we come to the final desert crossing. Moses is about to die. Most of us don't like to think about death. Comedian Woody Allen quipped, "I'm not afraid of death. I just don't want to be there when it happens." Yet no one can keep the Grim Reaper at bay.

One day both the great and small will stand before God to give an account. It won't matter how impressive we were down here. But it will matter what happens on the other side of the finish line.

Yet there is so little focus today on finishing well. On the eve of his martyrdom, St. Paul wrote in 2 Timothy 4:6&7, "The time has come for my departure. I have fought the good fight. I have finished the race. I have kept the faith." Surely Moses could have said the same thing. The thing we should fear most is that our life's work could be exposed to be as fraudulent as that of Shah Jahan. That's why we must learn this final principle of the desert crossings:

DO NOT FEAR DEATH SO MUCH AS THE INADEQUATE LIFE.

The obituary for Moses is written in the 34th chapter of Deuteronomy. After forty years of crossing the most desolate string of deserts on planet earth, he has brought his people to the edge of their Promised Land. It's been a gut-wrenching ultra-marathon, but he's finished his course.

Now he begins the walk to his gravesite. Death is the last and loneliest desert we will ever cross. As he trudges up the rocky spine of Mount Nebo, Moses pauses every so often to catch his breath and look back at the camp below. It is getting smaller with every step he takes, and he's feeling lonelier with each look back. He has loved these people for forty years. Now he's going off to die alone. The desert winds carry laughter of children and the playful banter of families gathered around distant campfires. But Moses won't be joining them this evening, or ever again.

Finally, he reaches the summit. It seems that the most significant moments of his life have been on mountaintops. He gazes at the Promised Land opposite the Jordan. He's so tantalizingly close, and yet he might as well be a million miles away. From the mountaintop, he sees both the success and failure of his life.

With dogged determination and faith, he has forged a nation out of a ragtag rabble of slaves and led them to the land of promise. Yet, because of the one great sin in his life, he is not allowed to go into the Land. It must be maddening to come so far, and yet fall so short; to put up with so much, and yet fail to grasp what you wanted most.

We can all identify with Moses. Life is littered with regrets. We could all admit that there is more than one Promised Land we never entered. Like Moses, our lives are a mixed bag. We don't know what he's thinking as he stands on the last mountaintop of life. But, as we stand alongside him, we remember all the times we've stumbled along the way. Like Moses, we want to finish well. As we walk with Moses to his grave, we learn some valuable lessons about crossing the finish line strong:

1) DEATH KEEPS ITS APPOINTMENTS. IT NEVER BARGAINS.

Deuteronomy 34:7 is profoundly significant for us all: "Moses was a hundred and twenty years old when he died, yet his eyes were not weak nor his strength gone." Moses did not die from natural causes. He still had a lot of mileage left in the tank. Even at 120 years of age, he's not ready to die.

Yet, death comes anyway. Hebrews 9:27 says, "...just as man is destined to die once, and after that to face the judgment..." Two facts are clear: death is our destiny and heaven's judgment is our destination. The King James Version of Hebrews 9:27 says, "It is appointed unto a man once to die..." The Greek word for appointed has the sense of exactness. In Psalm 139:16 David cries out to God, "All the days ordained for me were written in your book before one of them came to be." The Psalmist is saying that, before we were ever born, God had already written in our date book the exact number of days we would live. Ecclesiastes 9:12 says, "No one knows when his hour will come." But the exact year, month, week, day, hour, minute, and second has already been set.

We try to postpone it by healthy living. When someone asked Bob Hope the secret to his long life, he said, "I get my exercise by being a pall bearer for all my friends who died of heart attacks while jogging." Comedian George Carlin said it best: "If no one knows when a person is going to die, how can we say he died prematurely?" The truth is: no one dies prematurely. There is a profound line from Luigi Pirandello's Henry IV: "As soon as one is born, one starts dying." Heaven's clock is ticking. One day we will cross the great divide and answer for what we have done on this side.

2) IT'S BETTER TO LEARN HOW TO DIE THAN TO LIVE

Now we come to Moses' funeral. There is nothing better than going to a funeral. The wisest man who ever lived wrote in Ecclesiastes 7:1&2,

"A good name is better than fine perfume, and the day of death is better than the day of birth. It is better to go to the house of mourning than to go to the house of feasting for death is the destiny of every man; the living should take this to heart."

Solomon says three things in this snippet from Ecclesiastes: 1) the most important thing you can strive for is a good name; 2) if you want to develop the character that gives you a good name, attend some funerals. They will do more for you than parties or feasts; 3) because death is the destiny of everyone, we should take it seriously while we still have time.

At a funeral you realize that some day you too will die and people are going to gather together to remember you. What will they say? What legacy will you leave behind?

A young pastor conducted his first funeral in a small country church. Not knowing the deceased, he asked if someone would say something. No one responded. Again he asked for someone to speak up, but no one stirred. The young preacher was desperate.

"Would someone please give a good word about our departed brother!"
Again, stone-faced silence. Finally he said, "I will not end this service until someone speaks."
At last an old farmer got up, cleared his throat and said, "Well, he weren't as bad as his brother Bobby."

Not everyone is remembered well in death. The famous lawyer Clarence Darrow once quipped, "I have never wanted to see anyone die, but there are a few obituary notices I have read with pleasure." I hope that the four things that were said of Moses will be stated about us in our obituary:

MOSES LEFT WITHOUT LONELINESS

At first glance his death seems so pitifully lonely. He dies alone in the desert badlands of Moab. No one is there to comfort him during his last gasps of breath. No one dresses his remains, lays them in a casket, gives a eulogy, sings a hymn, or says a prayer over his gravesite.

Perhaps God wants to remind us of a harsh reality: even in the most peaceful death surrounded by loved ones, we will face a stark moment of loneliness. It's the moment we all fear most—when we say our final goodbye to this world and let go of everything and everyone we have ever known. We go naked and alone into the great beyond.

The French philosopher Albert Camus called it terrifying loneliness. The most ardent atheist is not sure at that moment. What if he gambled everything on nothing and finds God on the other side? The 70s rock band Three Dog Night expressed this angst in a golden oldie: "I know there ain't no heaven, but I hope there ain't no hell."

On the other hand, even the most ardent believers have a flicker of unspoken doubt. Will the belief on which they hung their eternal hope be vindicated on the other side? There is a terrifying loneliness in dying and going to a place we have never been. But Moses was not alone. Deuteronomy 34:5&6 say,

> "And Moses the servant of the LORD died there in Moab as the LORD had said. He buried him in Moab, the valley opposite Beth Peor, but to this day no one knows where his grave is."

He may have been alone when he breathed his last, but heaven was there to embrace him a millisecond after death. The words of British hymn-writer, John Oxenham say it best: "Death begins at life's first breath. And life begins at the touch of death."

The angels were watching when Moses breathed his last. In verse nine of his little New Testament book, Jude gives a curious insight into Moses' death. The archangel Michael wrestled with the fallen angel Lucifer for the body of Moses. Michael won that day. In our imagination, we can see that great angel tenderly carrying the limp body of the old man to a desert grave that God himself has already dug? Imagine a funeral where angels are pallbearers, angelic choirs sing, and God speaks a eulogy over the body, "Well done, good and faithful servant." It beats the Taj Mahal every day.

I Thessalonians 4:13 says to Christians, "...do not grieve like the rest of men who have no hope..." We do not go alone to misty shadow lands between here and heaven. Like Moses, an angel will be waiting to carry us into God's presence.

Jesus tells the story about a beggar named Lazarus who sat in rags outside the rich man's house, begging for scraps while dogs licked sores. Yet Luke 16:22 says, "The time came when the beggar died and the angels carried him to Abraham's side."

There will be no loneliness for believers. At their last breath, the door to heaven opens and angels carry them home. It doesn't matter what kind of memorial service is going on back home. The believer enters into the joyful company of Abraham and the saints who have gone on before! Heavenly choirs sing songs of celebration. God is there to speak the greatest eulogy of all: "Well done good and faithful servant. Enter into the joy of your Master's presence."

MOSES LEFT A LOSS

Deuteronomy 34:0 says, "The Israelites grieved for Moses in the plains of Moab thirty days, until the time of weeping and mourning was over." It is ironic that these people who had dogged Moses with complaints for forty years should now experience so much pain at his passing. They couldn't live with him, but now they can't live without him.

Every leader can learn a powerful lesson in the grief of his followers. Moses never tried to placate them like his brother Aaron did. He didn't try to be their best buddy, or win their popularity. He didn't pander to their felt needs, but he delivered what they really needed—even when they didn't want it.

Moses always spoke the truth to a people who were always ready to believe a lie. He was faithful when everyone else was unfaithful. He doggedly plodded forward when everyone else wanted to go back to Egypt. He stood strong when others faltered. Moses teaches us that children don't need moms and dads to be their good buddies; they need strong role models who will draw boundaries and get them through tough times. Church folks don't need pastors who make them feel good and get them out on time; they need men of compelling vision and uncompromising truth who will call them to transformed lives. Citizens don't need politicians who pander to their basest instincts; they are desperate for strong statesmen who will call them to blood, sweat, and tears.

Moses was a strong leader, a faithful friend, and someone who loved his people through thick and thin. He made a significant difference in their lives, and left a yawning hole behind, because he was a person of character. When we bring grace and holiness to our world, it will be much the poorer when we leave.

MOSES LEFT A LEADER

Deuteronomy 34:9 goes on to say, "Now Joshua son of Nun was filled with the spirit and wisdom because Moses had laid his hands on him. So the Israelites listened to him and did what the Lord had commanded Moses." Joshua was one of Moses' greatest gifts to his people.

Joshua was a young man when Moses first laid eyes on him. The old prophet saw something special in the young warrior. So he took him under his wings, and invested the next forty years in Joshua. He also poured his life into Joshua's best friend, Caleb. In short, Moses invested his life in the next generation.

He understood that life is a relay race. It's not enough to run our leg of the race and then celebrate our individual achievement. Unless we can pass on to those who follow behind what you received from those who came before us, we have not finished well.

Shah Jahan built a magnificent monument, but it was empty. If we invest in things rather than people, our lives are as hollow as the Taj Mahal. Before he died, U.S. Senator Paul Tsongas looked back over his impressive achievements. But he was sad because he had sacrificed his family to gain political power and prestige. He said to a reporter, "No one on his deathbed ever said, 'I wish I had spent more time in my business.'"

We will cross over to heaven stark naked. Nothing material that we leave behind will last. Recently, the government of India announced that the Taj Mahal is sinking into the earth. Some day it will collapse. Shah Jahan built a monument to his own narcissistic grief. In the end, he couldn't even find the remains of the wife for which he built his mosque. But it didn't matter. The monument had become an obsession fueled by pride.

A lot of people say that they are working for their families, or building churches for the glory of God, or piling up resources to help others; but they are really in it for their own fulfillment. On his deathbed, the Shah complained that his children hated him and none of them was a worthy successor. Centuries ago, his dynasty died and today he has no known descendants.

Only people will cross over to heaven. You can only take yourself, your family, and those you influence for heaven. Moses left behind a strong leader to take his people into the future. In a culture that mortgages its children's future, we do well to remember that Moses invested his best in the next generation.

MOSES LEFT A LEGACY

Deuteronomy 34 ends with his obituary in verses 10-12:

> "Since then, no prophet has risen in Israel like Moses, whom the Lord knew face to face, who did all those miraculous signs and wonders the Lord sent him to do in Egypt—to Pharaoh and to all his officials and to his whole land. For no one has ever shown the mighty power or performed the awesome deeds that Moses did in the sight of all Israel."

There's a lot of talk today about leaving a legacy. Since the earliest times, people etched crude paintings on their cave walls, Egyptian pharaohs built pyramids, and ordinary people left behind gravestones etched with their names—all screaming, "Remember that I once walked the face of this earth!"

Reduced to its lowest common denominator, the Taj Mahal is really the cry of a man who wanted the world to remember that he once loved a woman more than life itself. We still build our Taj Mahals: our careers, companies, homes, and churches. We leave scholarships in our name, and do philanthropic deeds as a lasting legacy to our fleeting presence on this earth.

Maybe all our talk about leaving is indicative of our narcissistic age. Moses never thought about leaving a legacy. If you read his obituary you will see one thing that jumps out: he was an obedient servant willing to labor in humble obscurity. He had an intimate relationship with God that could be described as "face to face." Because he obeyed God in impossible situations, he performed impossible miracles.

His life was so well lived that it left a lasting impression on those who watched him. He left no stone monuments behind to mark his time here. His memorials were made of flesh and bone—the lives of people he influenced. God wrote his obituary in Holy Writ. His life was etched in generations that followed. And 2,000 years later he stood in the Promised Land on Mt. Tabor, in all his resurrected glory, next to His LORD and Savior Jesus Christ. Legacies don't come to those who seek them. They are left quite by accident as a result of lives that seek to honor the LORD. May we do the same at the end of our last desert crossing called death.

DESERT REFLECTIONS

For eighty years Moses crossed a string of deserts. We have seen fourteen of those deserts ending with the last and loneliest—death.

How will you finish? In the 18th Century, a Scottish Presbyterian preacher got caught in a violent storm. He stopped by a cottage, and asked for shelter from the rain. As he sat by the fireplace, he saw a dying man laid out on a table and moaning in terror. The preacher crept up beside the old man and whispered the gospel in his ear. The man received Christ, and then he died. After he returned home, the preacher said to his wife,

"I saw a wondrous thing last night. I found a man in the state of sin. I saw him in the state of grace. I left him in the state of glory!"

Much is said today about getting started, but little about finishing well. Remember, you have reached your Promised Land when you are fully transformed into the image of Christ. The deserts transform you gradually by stripping away creation's allure and forcing you to turn to your Creator. In focusing on him, you will be fully like him after you cross your final desert.

CHRISTIAN'S TRANSFORMATION

EPILOGUE

"We delight in the beauty of the butterfly, but rarely admit the changes it had to go through to achieve that beauty."

Maya Angelou

Christian Dance spent his whole life in a desert crossing.

Cancer had come calling early. During the precious few years allotted him, Christian endured enough pain for several lifetimes. At age six, he had wasted away to skin and bones. The doctors warned his grieving parents that time was running out for their brave little boy.

It was during Christian's final days that nature bestowed its annual miracle on Northeast Oklahoma. Countless millions of yellow butterflies invaded Tulsa with a gentle firestorm of vibrant color and aerobatic dance. These monarchs of the near heavens covered the trees and fields, bringing unbridled joy after the grey bleakness of the Oklahoma winter.

But this gift seldom lasted more than a week or so. The yearly exodus of yellow butterflies left as suddenly as it came, moving on with the north winds.

A friend accompanied me to the hospital to visit Christian. Though most of the butterflies had already disappeared, she had managed to trap one that lagged behind. She thought its beauty might give a bit of joy to a dying boy.

Christian held the jar and peered at the imprisoned butterfly. A single tear ran down his cheek. With a grimace, he handed the jar to Marsha and whispered,

"Mommy, please set him free. He looks too much like me, caught in a place that he doesn't like to be."

Marsha took the lid off the jar as I pulled up the window in the hospital room. The butterfly escaped and joyfully fluttered through the open window, soaring away to freedom.

The dying boy watched intently until he could no longer see the butterfly. A profound silence fell on a hospital room that now seemed more like a cathedral. We all sensed that something sacred had just taken place. Then a wistful smile crossed Christian's face and he softly said to his mother,

"Someday soon, I'm going to be like that butterfly when I leave this body and fly away to Jesus in heaven."

Christian died a few days later. There are few events filled with more anguish than a child's funeral. After it was over, Gary and Marsha dreaded going back to their little house filled with memories of Christian. So a friend bundled them in his car and drove them home.

As the car turned into the long driveway, the most amazing sight greeted them. The lawn on both sides of the gravel road was covered with a carpet of yellow butterflies. As the car moved slowly down the driveway, they rose by the thousands and filled the skies with frenzied aerobatic dance.

Marsha jumped out of the car and ran into their swirling midst. For a joyous moment swarms of butterflies danced around her. During that magical moment, she forgot her grief and began to laugh with childish delight. Then the ballet of the butterflies abruptly ended as they rose in masse to catch the north wind.

Grief returned as quickly as it had left, and Marsha once again stood alone in the empty yard where her little boy had once played. Then a solitary butterfly returned and landed gently on her nose. For the longest time it sat there, its wings gently caressing her tear-stained cheeks. Then it rose on yellow butterfly wings and fluttered away to rejoin its companions.

Nature has no explanation for thousands of butterflies awaiting a grieving mother two weeks after the annual migration had flown north. Marsha was convinced that the butterfly that came back to caress her face was the one released from the jar in the hospital room. To this day, all those who were in that driveway are sure that they witnessed a miracle. God had orchestrated this dance of the butterflies to remind those grief-stricken parents about the hopeful words that their dying boy had uttered during his final days in the hospital:

"Someday soon, I'm going to be like that butterfly when I leave this body and fly away to Jesus in heaven."

Christian Dance was transformed, and every Christian will one day dance in the presence of their Savior and Lord. In your desert crossings, hold tightly to the Apostle Paul's promise to suffering Christians everywhere:

"And we, who with unveiled faces all reflect the Lord's glory, are being transformed into his likeness with ever-increasing glory..."

2 Corinthians 3:18

The word Paul used for "transformed" is the origin of our word metamorphosis, the process whereby a crawling caterpillar becomes a beautiful butterfly that soars on wings through the heavens. It is an amazing and yet painful process.

The caterpillar secretes liquid that stiffens into a silk like thread, with which it spins a cocoon around itself. It has literally created its own coffin. Inside its hardened chrysalis, the caterpillar is transformed into a pupa. The old caterpillar has now died to become a baby butterfly. But, before it will be strong enough to fly, it must go through the painful process of breaking out of its cocoon coffin. This process can take from ten days to several months of exhausting work. It is through this painstaking effort that the butterfly is made strong enough to soar.

Literally, the butterfly is transformed by tribulation.

Paul painted a magnificent portrait of the Christian life. We were once like caterpillars crawling along the face of the earth, eating the dust of this creation. But, in Christ, we died and were born again. Now we are going through the process of transformation. It is a re-creation borne of suffering. Cancer was Christian Dance's desert crossing. His death would also take his family across deserts of disappointment, grief and loneliness.

But that six year old boy knew what many adults have yet to figure out: one day he would soar like a butterfly to heaven. And so will all of us who are willing to cross the desert with Jesus.

When you get weary and discouraged, remember Christian Dance and the butterfly. Remember also, St. Paul's words, "...we are being transformed into his likeness with ever increasing glory..." Keep crossing your deserts. A Promised Land is waiting beyond them.

Then dear Christian, you too will dance on wings of glory.